D0438860

SELECTING A PRESIDENT

ALSO BY ELEANOR CLIFT

Two Weeks of Life: A Memoir of Love, Death, and Politics

Founding Sisters and the Nineteenth Amendment

War Without Bloodshed

Madam President: Women Blazing the Leadership Trail

Madam President: Shattering the Last Glass Ceiling

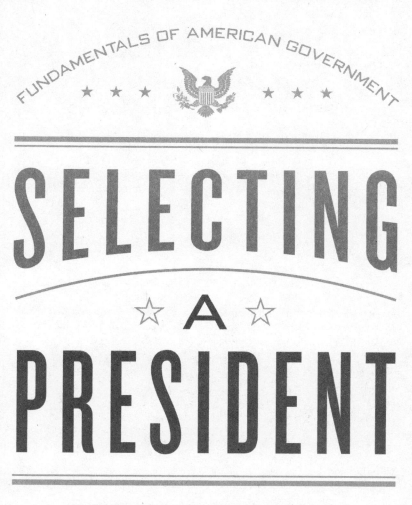

FUNDAMENTALS OF AMERICAN GOVERNMENT

★ ★ ★ ★ ★ ★ ★ ★

SELECTING

☆ A ☆

PRESIDENT

ELEANOR CLIFT
and MATTHEW SPIELER

Thomas Dunne Books
St. Martin's Press
New York

THOMAS DUNNE BOOKS.
An imprint of St. Martin's Press.

SELECTING A PRESIDENT. Copyright © 2012 by Eleanor Clift and Matthew Spieler.
All rights reserved. Printed in the United States of America. For information, address
St. Martin's Press, 175 Fifth Avenue, New York, N.Y. 10010.

www.thomasdunnebooks.com
www.stmartins.com

Design by Steven Seighman

Library of Congress Cataloging-in-Publication Data

Clift, Eleanor.
    Selecting a president / Eleanor Clift and Matthew Spieler.—1st ed.
      p. cm.
    ISBN 978-1-250-00449-9 (hardback)   4871 8752 6/13
    ISBN 978-1-4668-0223-0 (e-book)
  1. Presidents—United States—Election.   2. Presidents—United States—
Nomination.   3. Political campaigns—United States.   4. United States—Politics
and government.   I. Spieler, Matthew.   II. Title.
    JK528.C55 2012
    324.973—dc23

                                                                    2012008975

First Edition: May 2012

10 9 8 7 6 5 4 3 2 1

ELEANOR CLIFT
To all the history and civics teachers for their efforts in building citizen awareness

MATTHEW SPIELER
To my mother, Gene; and to my father, Francis Joseph, who taught me how to write

☆ CONTENTS ☆

☆ ACKNOWLEDGMENTS ☆

I would like to thank all the politicians whose lives and careers I have been privileged to report on. They taught me more than any textbook, and whatever their flaws, they dared to enter the arena.

—Eleanor Clift

I am grateful to my wife, Shannon, whose suggestions and editing, and whose love and support were invaluable. I am grateful also to my parents, who instilled in me the importance of political knowledge and awareness.

—Matthew Spieler

SELECTING

☆ A ☆

PRESIDENT

E very presidential election changes the course of history. To be sure, not all elections are equally consequential. But every presidential election—even those that might appear to revolve around trivial matters—has the potential to radically transform the politics of the United States.

Consider the 2000 election. That presidential contest was frequently derided as not only dull, but also for lacking a clear contrast between the two major candidates, Texas Governor George W. Bush and Vice President Al Gore. Yet the Bush presidency—perhaps the most controversial since that of Richard M. Nixon—radically reshaped American foreign policy. The Bush era was shaped by two wars, one in Afghanistan that is ongoing as of this writing, and the conflict in Iraq that lasted nearly a decade, cost thousands of American lives, and bitterly divided the country.

The George W. Bush era came to an end in the midst of a financial crisis that has mired the United States in a deep recession. Though the crisis may have been a boon politically to Barack Obama in 2008, persistently high unemployment and economic pessimism threatens to bring about his defeat in 2012.

In a sense, presidential elections are simple affairs. They usually feature two candidates from the same two political parties, running on policy platforms that are often very similar to those of their predecessors.

Most Americans only see a small snippet of each presidential election—a fragment of the larger story of each campaign. Most Americans begin to pay attention to presidential races in the final weeks before Election Day, which can be years after they began in earnest. This book offers a complete but concise guide to the nuts and bolts of presidential campaigns from start to finish—from a candidate's first trip to Iowa through the inauguration of a new president. It explains the features, structures, and institutions that shape presidential campaigns, from caucuses and pledged delegates to the Electoral College. We begin with the primary season and move through the nominating conventions, the general election campaign, Election Day, and end with the inauguration of the president-elect.

While each presidential campaign can be seen as a self-contained story with a beginning, middle, and end, each also includes smaller narratives within larger historical struggles. Characters who play a minor role in one election may play a prominent or even crucial part in future elections. One such example—examined in this book—is Hubert Humphrey's 1948 speech before the Democratic National Convention. Humphrey, the mayor of Minneapolis and future giant of Democratic politics, pled passionately for the Democratic Party to repudiate segregation and sever its ties to a constituency rooted in racial intimidation and violence. Despite Humphrey's efforts, racist elements would endure within Democratic politics for decades to come. But a Democratic president would sign civil rights legislation in 1964, cementing that party's transformation from a safe harbor for racist politics into a force for equality. Moreover, Humphrey's speech can be understood now as the beginning of a political realignment that radically reshaped American politics.

Those who follow politics closely often lament the apathy of the American public. Some blame a lack of civics education in modern public schooling. Many high school graduates have never taken a course that devotes any attention to presidential elections and why they are important. It is our hope that this book illustrates why presidential elections are so compelling. Presidential elections matter. They are *always* of critical importance. Quite simply, they affect all of our lives.

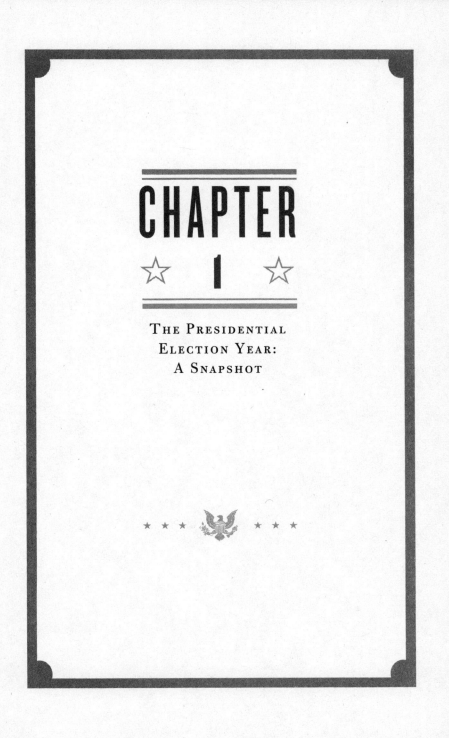

CHAPTER ☆ 1 ☆

THE PRESIDENTIAL
ELECTION YEAR:
A SNAPSHOT

On a Tuesday evening in early November, Americans gather in front of their television sets for the grand finale of a political drama years in the making. Once every four years, the usual sitcoms, primetime dramas, and reality shows give way to special news coverage: America is electing a new president.

As Election Night unfolds, a map of the United States begins to take shape. States won by Democrats are colored in blue, while those won by Republicans are shaded red. Sometimes, the night unfolds at an agonizingly slow pace.

The first news of the night usually trickles in around 7 p.m., after a few states with early poll closings report their results. Vermont's three electoral votes, not surprisingly, go to one party. The other standard-bearer wins Kentucky, as expected. An hour or two later, if all goes smoothly and it's not an especially close election, the networks declare winners in Pennsylvania, Ohio, and Michigan, and the outcome becomes clearer.

Election night can be filled with drama and surprises. Some candidates will win states they were projected to lose, and vice versa. Alternatively, Election Night can be a rather dull affair, as the outcome may not have been in doubt for months leading up to the voting.

On Election Day, the presidency is far from the only important political office up for grabs. All members of the House of Representatives and roughly one third of U.S. senators must also stand for election on that same day. But in presidential election years, the race for the White House is undoubtedly the main event.

Election Day in the United States is the culmination of a long, grueling process that tests those who seek the highest office in the land—and the leadership of the free world. While most Americans may only have been paying attention to the campaign for a matter of weeks, it has, in fact, been more than two years in the making.

Mere days after a new president takes office (or returns to office if he was reelected) the media turns its attention to the next campaign. Whether they're reporters, bloggers, or talking heads, the media will pontificate about what the next campaign will look like. Familiar names are mentioned, and leading critics of the president will give speeches and interviews in which they try to assume the leadership of the "loyal opposition."

Two years into a president's term, the presidential race comes into clearer focus. Following the midterm elections (which occur every two years, and in which members of both houses of Congress, as well as governors and state legislatures are elected), presidential aspirants form what are called "exploratory committees." Exploratory committees allow candidates to test the waters for a national campaign. At this early stage of a campaign, presidential hopefuls hire pollsters who gauge their popularity, and meet with local elected officials and political activists around the country. They raise money—and they will need to raise a lot of it in order to be taken seriously as a viable candidate to carry the Democratic or Republican banner in the presidential election.

There are, of course, third parties and independent candidates who run under no party label at all. Occasionally, these independent candidates have a major impact on the presidential race. By advocating such progressive policies as an eight-hour workday and voting rights for women, Teddy Roosevelt's Bull Moose Party garnered 27 percent of the vote in 1912, insuring the defeat of Republican president Howard Taft and helping to elect Democrat Woodrow Wilson. In 1992, third party candidate Ross Perot (who ran under the Reform Party banner) received nearly 20 percent of the vote. However, every U.S. president has been a Democrat or Republican since 1857. Thus, for all intents and purposes, voters have two major political parties from which to choose their president.

Some argue that third party candidates play the role of "spoiler." (In elections, the term "spoiler" refers to a candidate who has little or no chance of winning but draws enough votes away from a major candidate to cost him the election.) While the chances of a third party candidate winning the presidency may be remote, these dark horses can have an impact at the margins. For example, many Democrats still believe that Ralph Nader's share of the vote in Florida cost Al Gore the presidency in 2000. Nader ran under the Green Party banner, and attracted support from disaffected liberals who believed Gore had failed to stand up for progressive ideals.

This early period of the campaign marks the beginning of the "primary season." During the primaries, each state holds its own election. In closed primaries, voters choose from their own party. Registered Democratic voters choose from a field of Democratic candidates. Republican voters, meanwhile, vote for their preferred politician among an exclusively Republican field of candidates.

The rules governing the primaries vary by state. In New York, for example, only Democratic voters may vote in the Democratic primary, while the Republican primary is closed to all except registered Republican voters. In New Hampshire's "open primary," however, independent voters (who are not registered with either party) can vote in whichever primary they choose. (Of course, even in open primaries, voters may only cast one ballot—they may vote in either the Democratic or the Republican primaries, but *not* both contests.)

Fourteen states—Alaska, Colorado, Idaho, Kansas, Minnesota, North Dakota, Iowa, Nevada, Nebraska, Washington, Maine, Wyoming, Texas, and Utah hold "caucuses" on Election Day, where political activists assemble to openly lobby for candidates and divvy up their support. The Iowa caucuses kick off the primary season and have achieved outsized influence in the presidential selection process for the small, mostly rural state. Texas also has a primary, making it the only state where residents can legally vote twice.

Early "straw polls" shape perceptions of the strength of the various candidates, but are not binding. The Ames, Iowa, straw poll on behalf of the Republican Party is the most famous. Held on a Saturday in August the year before the election, it has become a costly venture for candidates who build their numbers by busing people in and providing free food and entertainment. GOP frontrunner Mitt Romney, who spent more than a million dollars to win a narrow victory in 2007, skipped the Iowa caucus in 2011, ceding prime space in the arena to Representative Ron Paul, who paid $31,000 to the Republican state party for the honor.

By campaigning during the primaries, candidates are vying to win delegates from each state. The ultimate goal is to win enough delegates to clinch the Democratic or Republican nomination. After all of the primary elections and caucuses are over, each political party holds a convention and nominates the candidate who receives the support of the most delegates. (This process is actually more complicated, and will be explained in greater detail later.)

By the end of the primary season, voters in every state of the Union (as well as territories such as Puerto Rico) have cast their votes for the nominees of America's two major political parties. Only after every state has completed this process can the general election begin in which the Democratic candidate faces off against the Republican.

After the Democratic and Republican parties nominate their candidates, in late August and early September, the general election begins in earnest. The two candidates "barnstorm the country," standard-bearers for America's two major political philosophies in a battle for control of the White House. The Republican will run on a platform of lower taxes, scaling back or eliminating some programs, and less government regulation of business and financial dealings. The Democrat generally runs on a platform of maintaining or perhaps expanding the social safety net, aid to the poor, environmental protection, and support for organized labor. Differences over foreign policy can also define the two candidates. Republicans are often seen as backing a more hawkish, aggressive foreign policy that emphasizes military strength, while the Democrat might be more inclined to emphasize international cooperation and diplomacy.

Following the two parties' conventions, the general election kicks into high gear. Both candidates spend their time campaigning almost exclusively in states that are considered "toss-ups," or "swing states"—in other words, states that do not lean strongly toward one political party in presidential elections. The Democratic candidate, for example, will not campaign in heavily Democratic Massachusetts during the general election. The

Republican will not waste time campaigning in Idaho, which is safely Republican.

Ohio residents, meanwhile, will see a lot of both candidates. So will Pennsylvanians, Michiganders, and Floridians. Meanwhile, the voters of Vermont, New York, Hawaii, Alaska, and South Carolina are all but forgotten, as their votes are seldom seen as up for grabs.

During this period of the campaign—usually in late September and October—the presidential candidates will participate in a live, nationally televised debate. While these debates rarely doom a candidate or rescue him from a badly ailing campaign—they can prove to be consequential. Just weeks before voters go to the polls, viewer perceptions of presidential candidates take shape and solidify as the two contenders go toe-to-toe.

On Election Day, presidential campaigning comes to an end. (The Constitution requires that Election Day be held on the first Tuesday after the first Monday in November.) Voters go to the polls and later settle into their living rooms to watch the election returns on television. The two candidates, with much fanfare, visit their local polling place and wave to the cameras before casting their ballot—presumably for themselves. Then they retreat into seclusion with their families and closest advisors until a winner is declared. At last, it is time to give a victory or concession speech.

Once the presidential election has a clear victor, the loser concedes defeat. He graciously calls on his supporters to stand behind the nation's new president. The winner—now the "president-elect"—attempts to rally the entire country behind him and prepares for a transition. This transition, in which one presidential administration passes the reins of power to the next, begins the day after the election and culminates with the new president being sworn into office on January 20. On that day—Inauguration Day—the president-elect gives a speech before both houses of Congress, various dignitaries, and the public, and takes the presidential oath of office. At the conclusion of that oath, the president-elect becomes the president of the United States.

To recap, there are essentially five stages of presidential elections:

STAGE I (JANUARY–AUGUST)—The primaries, in which the two political parties choose their candidates. (In reality, candidates begin campaigning in the primaries long before January, but the first caucus or primary election generally takes place during this month.

STAGE II (AUGUST–SEPTEMBER)—The political parties' conventions, in which the winners of the primaries are nominated for president.

STAGE III (SEPTEMBER–NOVEMBER)—The general election campaign, in which the winners of the primaries compete against each other. This part of the presidential campaign, for all intents and purposes, is usually a two-person race between a Democrat and a Republican.

STAGE IV (NOVEMBER)—Election Day.

STAGE V (JANUARY 20)—Inauguration Day—the newly elected president is sworn into office.

CHAPTER 2

THE PRIMARIES

I n the dead of winter, Iowans gather in local schools, libraries, and churches. At these small gatherings with their friends and neighbors, they debate the issues of the day: war, health care reform, education policy, taxes, and—most importantly—their preferred candidates for the highest office in the land. For years now, this marks the official kickoff of the "presidential primaries," in which Democratic and Republican voters choose their respective standard-bearers.

The small meetings, collectively, are the Iowa Caucuses—home to the first votes cast for president of the United States. These votes are a far cry from a secret ballot. Iowans not only cast their votes publicly, but also lobby undecided caucusgoers, and build coalitions to put their man or woman over the top. Iowa's first-in-the nation status during the primaries gives the state considerable influence over whom the two political parties choose as their presidential nominees.

For a brief period—perhaps from the late fall through the winter *preceding* an election year—Iowa becomes the center of the national media's attention. Vote-rich California and New York see little in the way of campaigning, while a Midwestern state perhaps known best for its corn becomes the focal point of the U.S. presidential election.

The Iowa Caucuses have catapulted dark horse candidates and contenders who were left for dead all the way to the nomination.

In the fall and winter of 2003, for example, former Vermont Governor Howard Dean looked to be riding a wave of liberal discontent to the Democratic nomination.

Shortly after the U.S.-led invasion of Iraq (which most Democratic presidential candidates supported), antiwar Democrats flocked to Dean—the only major candidate to oppose the war. Massachusetts Senator John Kerry, who had once been the presumptive frontrunner for the Democratic nomination, saw his support dwindle among rank and file Democrats. Political pundits declared his candidcy dead. But Iowa's "late-deciders" (previously undecided voters who make up their minds just before the caucuses begin) rallied to Kerry in the final days leading up to the vote. The Bay State Democrat's come-from-behind first place finish shocked the political establishment and propelled him to a victory in the New Hampshire primary (which follows the Iowa Caucuses) and eventually all the way to the nomination.[1]

Meanwhile, Senator John Edwards—a Democrat from North Carolina—surprised political observers by finishing second. Dean, meanwhile, finished a distant third and his campaign never recovered. (His only victory during the primary season was in his home state of Vermont, long after Kerry had locked up the Democratic nomination.)

The power of the Iowa Caucuses to winnow the field was perhaps most evident in the case of Representative Richard Gephardt, who represented a district in neighboring Missouri. Gephardt had run for president in 1988 and won the Iowa Caucuses. After a humiliating fourth place finish there in 2004, Gephardt abandoned his presidential ambitions for good.

Conventional wisdom once held that the presidential primaries only allowed for "three tickets" out of Iowa. These tickets were reserved for the winner, and the second and third place finishers. For years, a strong second or third place finish in Iowa could keep candidates in the running in future nominating contests. In 1972, George McGovern, a Democratic senator from South Dakota, navigated a successful path to the Democratic nomination after finishing third in Iowa and second in New Hampshire. Even though Maine Senator Ed Muskie actually won both the Iowa Caucuses and New Hampshire primary that year, his weaker-than-expected performance in those states damaged his campaign, and allowed McGovern to overtake him.

The Iowa Caucuses are also important because a victory or strong showing can boost a candidate who is unknown in much of the country. On January 3, 2008, Barack Obama—then a first term senator from Illinois—won an upset victory over front-runner Hillary Rodham Clinton, a second term senator from New York and former First Lady. Obama won Iowa by an 8-point margin, while Clinton finished a disappointing third behind Obama and John Edwards. Obama, aided by the positive media coverage that stems from a major electoral victory, quickly erased Clinton's lead in the national polls. He had proven he was a contender, and won over previously skeptical Democratic primary voters.

Yet a victory in Iowa is no guarantee of a sustained winning streak, much less the nomination. Obama soon learned this lesson when Clinton rallied to a surprising victory in New Hampshire, reclaiming the front-runner mantle. (A month later, in early February, Obama overtook Clinton in both delegates and public perception as the leading candidate for the Democratic nomination.[2])

Similarly, former Arkansas Governor Mike Huckabee won the Iowa Caucuses in the 2008 Republican primaries, but went on to lose the New Hampshire primary to Arizona Senator John McCain. While Huckabee did win a number of subsequent primaries (particularly in the South), he failed to mount a sustained, serious challenge to McCain for the nomination.[3]

Before going any further, we should clarify what it means to "win a primary." When the news media reports the election returns during the primaries, they declare the winner of a state's popular votes to be the "winner" of that state's primary. Yet the ultimate goal of winning primaries is to win enough *delegates* to win the nomination. For each state's primary or caucus, a certain number of delegates to the party convention are up for grabs. The candidate with the most delegates after all the primaries are over wins the nomination. But the rules governing how delegates are awarded to candidates differ from state to state, and have traditionally differed dramatically between the two parties.

Many Republican primaries have long awarded delegates to presidential candidates through a simple, winner-take-all system. (Iowa, New Hampshire, and South Carolina were notable exceptions to this rule. In those, states, the Republicans award delegates proportionally.) Thus, when John McCain won the New York primary in 2008, he was awarded all 101 of the Empire State's delegates.[4]

The Democrats, however, use a proportional representation system to award delegates to their presidential candidates. This system allocates delegates to candidates based on their share of the vote in each primary and caucus. However, the Democrats' proportional representation rule provides greater delegate representation to areas that have a history of strong support for Democratic candidates. Thus, Democratic strongholds are overrepresented in the delegate count. This led to a rather awkward scenario following the Nevada Democratic caucuses in 2008. While Hillary Clinton won the popular vote in that state, Barack Obama netted more delegates because he outperformed his rival in areas that had historically shown strong support for Democrats.[5]

The consequences of a winner-take-all system versus a proportional representation method were starkly illustrated during the 2008 primaries. While McCain won all of New York's delegates after winning its primary, New York Senator Hillary Rodham Clinton won only 139 of 232 of the state's delegates after carrying her home state by a 17-point margin. Obama, meanwhile, won 93 delegates from New York.

Thus, winning the popular vote made a great deal more difference in the 2008 Republican primaries than in the Democratic contests. After all of the primaries and caucuses had ended, John McCain had more than five times as many delegates as the second place finisher, Mike Huckabee. This was a direct result of McCain's triumphs in many winner-take-all contests. At the conclusion of the Democratic primaries, however, Barack Obama led Hillary Clinton by the slimmest of margins due to the Democrats' proportional representation system.

The Republican National Committee (RNC), however, changed its delegate apportionment rules before the 2012 presidential nominating contest. Taking a page out of the Democrats' playbook, the RNC required states holding primaries before April to allocate delegates through a proportional representation system—although states were given leeway with respect to the how such a proportional system would work. Needless to say, this is a marked departure from the manner in which Republicans nominated their candidates in the past, and has the potential to make it far more difficult for one candidate to lock down the nomination early in the primary season. (The RNC rules still allow states to hold "winner-take-all" contests beginning in April. Party leaders hoped that this would prevent a protracted fight for the GOP nomination lasting all the way into June.)

★ SUPER TUESDAY ★

While the Iowa caucuses and New Hampshire primary mark the much-anticipated kickoff of the presidential primary season, candidates rarely clinch the Democratic or Republican nomination before "Super Tuesday." On Super Tuesday, literally thousands of delegates are at stake. States across the country hold their primaries and caucuses, and all candidates who are still in the running make a mad dash to win over undecided voters.

Presidential contenders can knock their opponents out of the running with a strong showing on Super Tuesday, and even win the nomination outright. John Kerry clinched the Democratic nomination for president in 2004 after winning major contests across the country, including victories in New York, California, Ohio, Georgia, and his home state of Massachusetts. His last major rival for the Democratic nomination—North Carolina Senator John Edwards—conceded the race to Kerry the following day.

In 2000, then-Texas Governor George W. Bush fended off a spirited challenge on Super Tuesday from Arizona Senator John McCain by winning similarly sweeping victories in delegate-rich California, Missouri, New York, and Maryland. After winning just four New England states with the help of independent voters (those states held open primaries), McCain bowed out and conceded the nomination to Bush.[6]

More recently, however, Super Tuesday failed to produce the decisive victory that was both expected and predicted at the beginning of the 2008 primary season. In fact, Super Tuesday in

2008 was so "super" that it seemed virtually assured that the Democratic and Republican nominees would be effectively chosen on that night—February 1. On the Republican side, John McCain became, for all intents and purposes, the Republican nominee. While Arkansas Governor Mike Huckabee remained in the race after Super Tuesday, McCain was regarded as the presumptive nominee after winning enough delegates to clinch the nomination.

On the Democratic side, however, Super Tuesday ended in a draw—a photo finish between Hillary Rodham Clinton and Barack Obama. While Clinton prevailed in the major prizes of New York and California, Obama won 13 of the 22 contests— and trounced Clinton in the many states with fewer delegates, including Alaska, Idaho, Utah, Colorado, Kansas, and North Dakota. By winning landslide victories in smaller states—and winning his home state of Illinois by a two-to-one margin— Obama won 803 of all delegates up for grabs on Super Tuesday compared to Clinton's 799.[7]

With no clear winner on Super Tuesday, Clinton and Obama dueled until June 3, when he clinched the Democratic nomination after winning the Montana primary. After Obama had finally vanquished his Democratic rival, NBC political analyst Chuck Todd declared Obama's victory over Clinton to be the "the greatest political upset maybe in the history of American politics."[8]

★ POLITICAL PARTIES ★

The primaries are run by the two major political parties. Each makes its own rules with respect to nominating candidates. Before elaborating on the role of political parties in presidential elections, we should take a moment to understand the structure of those parties.

While the structure of political parties varies from state to state, they adhere to a similar design. At the bottom of the leadership pyramid are the local precincts. Precincts essentially refer to electoral districts within counties. Each precinct has a leader. In some states (and depending on which party they belong to), these leaders are known as precinct captains, precinct committeemen, or precinct committee officers. The precinct heads—who are often, but not always elected—are the political officials who are most in touch with the grass roots supporters of the party. These individuals hold meetings with voters and local party activists; distribute official, party-backed campaign literature at election time; and seek to register new eligible voters.

These local party officials represent their precincts at county committees. Each county committee has a chairman, who is active in both local and statewide party business.

States, meanwhile, have State Central Committees. The chairmen of state committees are professional political operatives. They take an active role in fundraising as well as statewide elections—including gubernatorial and U.S. Senate races, state legislative campaigns, and even presidential campaigns.

The Democratic National Committee (DNC) and Republican National Committee (RNC), meanwhile, are made up of state party officials. The national committees promote the two parties' platforms, raise money, and support candidates up and down the ballot on Election Day.

The chairmen of the two national committees also become spokesmen for their parties. They appear frequently on news and interview programs to make the case for their party and criticize their opponents.

When a political party holds the White House, the president chooses his party's national chairman behind the scenes. Technically, the committee must still formally elect the president's choice. In reality, the president enjoys a great deal of deference from his party's national committee.

The party out of power, however, often experiences an unpredictable and divisive campaign for the chairmanship of the national committee.

In the wake of Democrat John Kerry's loss to President George W. Bush in 2004, a raucous, bitter race for the DNC chairmanship ensued. Much of the Democratic Party's liberal wing—dominated by younger progressive activists—favored Howard Dean. Dean had fared badly in the Democratic primaries, finishing behind John Kerry and John Edwards. In the immediate aftermath of Kerry's defeat, Dean worked to build support among liberals for his campaign for DNC chair, promising to rebuild the party in regions where it was no longer competitive.

Dean vowed to send Democratic organizers to rock-ribbed Republican states like Mississippi and Utah to make the party's case. Dean's plan—known as the "50 State Strategy," came under attack from Democratic Party leaders in Congress who saw the plan as a foolish waste of time and resources. Focusing on places where Democratic candidates had no hope of winning threatened to divert resources from Democrats representing swing constituencies in the House and Senate, they argued.

Dean went on to win the chairmanship easily, and implemented his plan to extend the Democratic Party's reach beyond its traditional strongholds.[9] Still, Dean's critics were not won over. Rather, his election led to a major rift in the party's leadership that endured for more than two years.

In fact, the 50 State Strategy led to a long-running feud between Dean and another prominent party leader: Representative Rahm Emanuel (D-IL). Emanuel, who was leading the charge to return the House to Democratic control after twelve years of Republican rule, accused Dean of damaging the Democrats' chances to retake control of Congress.[10] (For the record, the Democrats did win control of Congress in 2006. Whether Dean or Emanuel deserves a greater share of the credit for this feat remains a point of contention among Democrats.)

The aftermath of Arizona Senator John McCain's loss to Barack Obama in the 2008 presidential election yielded a similar free-for-all on the Republican side. (President Obama installed his ally, Virginia Governor Tim Kaine, as the Democratic National Committee chairman.) Michael Steele, the former one-term lieutenant governor of Maryland, ran an insurgent, outsider's campaign for the RNC chairmanship.

Steele, who was vying to become the first African American RNC chair, argued that Republicans must reach out to black voters, a constituency that had supported Democrats in overwhelming numbers since President Lyndon B. Johnson signed the Civil Rights Act of 1964. Steele prevailed, defeating his last standing opponent—South Carolina Republican Party Chairman Katon Dawson—by a vote of 91–77. In his unsuccessful bid for RNC Chair, Dawson had been dogged by past comments criticizing school desegregation as well as his membership in an all-white country club.

Like Dean, Steele had a tempestuous relationship with the Republican Party's establishment leadership. Republican insiders viewed Steele, who was outspoken, blunt, and prone to verbal gaffs, as too much of a loose cannon to serve as an effective spokesman for the GOP.[11] Steele lost his bid for a second term as chairman.

★ THE ROLE OF THE NATIONAL COMMITTEES IN THE ★ PRESIDENTIAL PRIMARIES

While elections are primarily the responsibility of state governments and state political parties, the Democratic and Republican National Committees do play a part in laying the ground rules for primaries and caucuses that choose presidential nominees. In fact, they sometimes punish state political parties who violate the national party rules by trying to schedule early primary elections.

Iowa and New Hampshire have traditionally enjoyed "first-in-the-nation status" with respect to voting in the primary season—Iowa holds the nation's first caucuses, while New Hampshire is home to the first primary. Some state parties have tried to schedule earlier primaries to bring greater attention to their states. Many have argued that allowing Iowa and New Hampshire—with their predominantly white populations—to dominate the early (and often most crucial) stages of the primaries mutes the influence of African American and Latino voters, who make up a sizable share of the Democratic base.

In 2008, the Michigan and Florida Democratic parties sought to move their primaries up to give their states more influence in choosing the Democratic nominee for president. The Democratic National Committee had prohibited states from scheduling primaries before February 5—although Iowa, New Hampshire, South Carolina, and Nevada were exempted from this rule. Michigan and Florida scheduled their primaries for January 15 and January 28, respectively. While voters of those states went to the polls, their votes were not counted. Since their state parties had violated the rules, the Democratic National

Committee stripped Floridians and Michiganders of their delegates to the Democratic National Convention.[12]

★ PRESIDENTIAL CANDIDATES ★

A common joke among reporters covering Congress is that
every member of the U.S. Senate wakes up in the morning and
sees a future president in the mirror. Indeed, sometimes it seems
as though senators who have no presidential ambitions at all are
more remarkable than those harboring dreams of winning the
highest office in the land. Senators, however, are not the only
elected officials who use their office as a launching pad for a
presidential campaign. Governors frequently run. In fact, in the
presidential elections that took place from 1976 through 2004,
all but one of the victors were governors. (The exception was
President George H. W. Bush, who won the presidency after
serving two terms as vice president under Ronald Reagan—and
lost his reelection bid to Bill Clinton in 1992, who was then the
governor of Arkansas.)

Despite senators' famed hunger for the presidency, they rarely
win presidential elections. Until 2008, when then-Senator
Barack Obama won the White House, no one had been elected
president directly from the Senate since John F. Kennedy in
1960. (Although Lyndon B. Johnson had served as a senator
from Texas, he was elected in 1964 after having been president
for roughly fourteen months following Kennedy's assassination.)

Members of the House of Representatives frequently run for
president. Yet if history is any guide, their chances of winning are
even more remote than senators'. Only one sitting member of the
House of Representatives has ever been elected president: James
Garfield in 1880.[13] Members of the House who do run for presi-

dent are generally regarded as one-issue candidates, or "vanity candidates." Representative Dennis Kucinich, an Ohio Democrat, has run for president twice on a platform of staunch liberalism and government activism not seen since the Franklin Delano Roosevelt's New Deal. Representative Tom Tancredo (R-CO) ran for president in 2008 on an anti-immigration platform.

Representative Richard Gephardt, a Missouri Democrat, however, *was* regarded as a serious candidate for the presidency in 1988 and 2004. Yet he was not simply a rank-and-file member of the House—he was a member of the House Democratic leadership, and had served as the top House Democrat (House Minority Leader) from 1995 to 2003.

This is not to say that members of the House of Representatives don't *eventually* become president. Rather, the House is usually a stepping-stone on the way to the White House. Gerald Ford served as House Republican Leader before he was tapped as vice president by President Richard M. Nixon. When Nixon resigned due to the famous Watergate scandal, Ford succeeded him as president. Nixon himself had served in the House early in his political career. (He was then elected to the Senate from California, and later served as vice president under Dwight Eisenhower.) President George H. W. Bush served in the House before becoming vice president under Ronald Reagan and then winning the presidency in his own right in 1988. (Before becoming vice president, he had also served as an ambassador to the United Nations and as the director of the Central Intelligence Agency.)

Other presidents who once served in the House include Lyndon Johnson and John F. Kennedy. Thus, while many American presidents have once served in the House, very few were elected to the presidency directly from the chamber.[14] Rather, election to the House marked the beginning of their political ascent.

Members of the president's cabinet—such as secretaries of State or Defense—also sometimes seek the White House, although such candidacies are rare in recent history. The last cabinet member to be elected president was Herbert Hoover in 1928. Hoover had served as Secretary of Commerce in President Calvin Coolidge's cabinet. Such candidacies by cabinet members were far more common during the first few decades following the American Revolution. John Quincy Adams was secretary of state under President James Monroe for eight years before winning the presidency in 1824. Monroe, meanwhile, had served in President James Madison's cabinet as both secretary of state and secretary of war (a cabinet position that no longer exists).

Technically, vice presidents are members of the president's cabinet. Unlike all other cabinet members, however, they are not appointed. Rather, they are popularly elected along with the president.

Military leaders have also sought the presidency, although the last person with an exclusively military background to be elected president was Dwight D. Eisenhower in 1952. Back in 1868, General Ulysses S. Grant won the presidency after serving as Union military commander during the Civil War.

More recently, Wesley Clark—a former Supreme Allied Commander of NATO—sought the Democratic nomination for president in 2004. He was a minor factor in the campaign, however, and withdrew from the race after winning the Oklahoma primary—his only victory during the primaries.[15]

Thus, presidential candidates can come from just about any background imaginable. Those who are generally seen as viable presidential contenders, however, tend to be governors, vice presidents, or senators.

CHAPTER ☆ 3 ☆

THE CONVENTIONS: CLINCHING THE NOMINATION

I n late August of a presidential election year, the intraparty battles for the Democratic and Republican nominations come to an end. (In reality, candidates generally stop competing in the primaries much earlier—usually no later than June, and sometimes as early as February. Still, the primary campaign is technically not over until the two parties' conventions are completed, and nominees are chosen.)

★ WHO ARE DELEGATES AND WHERE DO THEY ★ COME FROM?

Delegates to the Democratic and Republican national conventions are elected during the primaries and caucuses, or chosen by state party committees. These delegates—known as "pledged delegates"—are elected or chosen during the primaries with the understanding that they will vote for a certain candidate at the national convention. However, those delegates are not required to vote for the candidates to whom they are pledged at the convention. In general, however, pledged delegates honor their commitments.

At the Democratic National Convention, pledged delegates make up 80 percent of the total delegate count. The remaining 20 percent are "superdelegates"—members of the House of

Representatives, senators, governors, former presidents, and other party leaders. (As of the 2008 presidential election, there were 795 superdelegates.) The superdelegates are unpledged and are free to support whomever they wish. The Republican National Convention does not make use of superdelegates. Republican conventions do, however, have 156 "automatic delgates," which serve a similar purpose.

The superdelegates have rarely played a significant role in the Democratic nominating process, but threatened to do so in 2008. With Clinton and Obama locked in a near tie among pledged delegates, political observers wondered what would happen if one candidate had won the pledged delegate count and the popular vote, but the superdelegates put the second place finisher over the top. In effect, the superdelegates would have overruled the Democratic primary electorate—and this could have led to a Democratic civil war between the Clinton and Obama factions. Such a scenario was avoided, however, since Obama—who led among pledged delegates—eventually surpassed Clinton among superdelegate support in May.

The superdelegates also played a prominent role during the 1984 Democratic presidential primaries. While former Vice President Walter Mondale won a plurality of pledged delegates, he failed to win an outright majority, and had to rely on superdelegates to put him over the top in his quest to be the Democratic nominee. Colorado Senator Gary Hart was Mondale's main rival in that campaign. Hart ran an insurgent campaign for the nomination, while Mondale was widely seen as the candidate with the backing of the Democratic establishment. Not surprisingly, the superdelegates—who, as senators, congressmen, etc., were largely establishment figures—threw their support to Mondale, thereby enabling him to clinch the Democratic nomination.[1]

★ THE PARTY PLATFORM ★

At the political parties' national conventions, delegates agree on a platform. The party platform is a manifesto of sorts; it is a statement of values and principles, and lays out the policy positions that make up the party's agenda. Of course, the nominees are by no means bound by these platforms. They are free to ignore or even violate them if they so choose. Still, the platform remains an important institution that has, over time, helped to define the two major political parties.

Of course, some platforms have proven more consequential than others. In 1948, the Democrats included support for civil rights in their party platform for the first time. Specifically, the liberal wing of the party proposed an end to school segregation, workplace discrimination, as well as federal antilynching legislation. (The first two proposals eventually became law in the mid-1960s. To this day, however, no federal antilynching legislation has been enacted.) Hubert Humphrey—then the mayor of Minneapolis—gave an impassioned speech imploring the convention to adopt the civil rights plank:

> There are those who say to you—we are rushing this issue of civil rights. I say we are 172 years late.
>
> There are those who say—this issue of civil rights is an infringement on states' rights. The time has arrived for the Democratic party to get out of the shadow of states' rights and walk forthrightly into the bright sunshine of human rights.[2]

Humphrey and his allies succeeded in including support for civil rights in the 1948 Democratic platform. This would help to bring about a realignment in American politics: The Democratic Party, long associated with southern politics, become closely associated with civil rights. And to this day, there is no constituency more loyal to the Democratic Party than African American voters. In 2000, Al Gore won 92 percent of the African American vote. In 2004, 88 percent of blacks voted for John Kerry. In 2008, Barack Obama carried a record 95 percent of the African American vote.[3]

While Humphrey helped put the Democratic Party firmly on the side of civil rights, the reaction among conservative southern Democrats was immediate, and signaled the beginning of the end of the Democrats' hold on the "Solid South." Southern conservatives, led by then-South Carolina Governor Strom Thurmond, walked out of the 1948 Democratic convention.

Many of those southerners would never return to the Democratic fold. Refusing to unite behind President Truman—who had embraced support for civil rights—the "States' Rights Democrats," or "Dixiecrats," nominated Thurmond for president in 1948. He carried four southern states in the general election. Over the next five decades, the South continued to slowly drift away from its Democratic roots—and eventually became the power base of the modern Republican Party.

The party platforms matter less today than they did in 1948, largely because political parties are far more cohesive in the modern political era. The Democrats no longer harbor reactionary segregationists in their coalition. While feuds undoubtedly persist between the party's liberals, moderates, and conservatives, those feuds do not threaten to split the party, as occurred in 1948. The Republicans, meanwhile, have also become more cohesive. With its northern liberal wing almost extinct, it has become a far more conservative coalition.

In 2008, the Democratic Platform included a commitment to universal health care—the cornerstone of Barack Obama's domestic agenda: "If one thing came through in the platform hearings, it was that Democrats are united around a commitment that every American man, woman, and child be guaranteed affordable, comprehensive healthcare. In meeting after meeting, people expressed moral outrage with a health care crisis that leaves millions of Americans—including nine million children—without health insurance and millions more struggling to pay rising costs for poor quality care. Half of all personal bankruptcies in America are caused by medical bills. We spend more on health care than any other country, but we're ranked forty-seventh in life expectancy and forty-third in child mortality."[4]

The 2008 Republican Platform included support for a constitutional amendment barring same-sex marriage: "Because our children's future is best preserved within the traditional understanding of marriage, we call for a constitutional amendment that fully protects marriage as a union of a man and a woman, so that judges cannot make other arrangements equivalent to it. In the absence of a national amendment, we support the right of the people of the various states to affirm traditional marriage through state initiatives."

The 2008 Republican platform also emphasized a commitment to gun owners and the second amendment: "We call on the next president to appoint judges who will similarly respect the Constitution. Gun ownership is responsible citizenship, enabling Americans to defend themselves, their property, and communities."[5]

★ THE RUNNING MATE: CHOOSING A VICE ★ PRESIDENTIAL CANDIDATE

In addition to nominating a candidate for president, convention delegates also nominate their party's candidate for vice president.

While a vice presidential candidate (also known in the political vernacular as the "veep") is technically selected by convention delegates, the choice for a vice presidential running mate has been the prerogative of the presidential nominee for the last half century. Adlai Stevenson (in 1956) was the last presidential nominee to allow a convention to choose his running mate.[6] (The last candidate to announce his running mate at the convention was Jimmy Carter in 1976, who selected Minnesota Senator Walter Mondale. Since then, presidential candidates have selected their running mates before the convention.)[7]

After presidential candidates have locked down enough delegates to be considered the "presumptive nominee," they turn their focus to the search for a running mate. Candidates often use a "search committee" to put together a list of names for the candidate and top aides to consider. In 2000, then-Texas Governor George W. Bush selected former Defense Secretary and Wyoming Congressman Dick Cheney to head his vice presidential search committee. Thus, political observers were surprised when Bush chose Cheney as his running mate. (This led some to joke that Cheney, when tasked with finding the best candidate to be vice president under Bush, chose himself.)[8]

Presidential candidates consider a number of factors when choosing a vice presidential running mate. A candidate's ability to balance the ticket from a regional or geographic perspective has long been important. This was especially true of Democratic candidates over the last half century; the enduring success of the

Democratic Party nationally depended on its ability to maintain a coalition of northern liberals and southern conservatives.

Thus, a northern presidential candidate generally looked for a southerner to balance the ticket. In 1960, John F. Kennedy—then a senator from Massachusetts—chose Lyndon Johnson of Texas (who had been the Democratic majority leader of the Senate) as his running mate. When a governor of Georgia by the name of Jimmy Carter was set to accept the Democratic nomination for president in 1976, he chose a northern liberal as his running mate: Senator Walter Mondale of Minnesota.

Regional balance, however, has become less important in recent years. In 1992, then-Arkansas Governor Bill Clinton chose fellow southerner Al Gore (who was a senator from Tennessee at the time) to be his running mate. Clinton, however, did not run as a Democrat in the "Southern Conservative" mold. Rather, he had been a leader in the "New Democrat" coalition—a new, "moderate" brand of Democrat that was neither liberal nor conservative. They tended to be socially progressive but emphasized fiscal conservatism.

In choosing running mates, presidential candidates must also take into account an ideological gap between the two people on the ticket. A few minor differences on various issues would normally not preclude someone from being seriously considered for the job. Such minor policy differences can be papered over during the campaign. A major ideological gulf between a presidential candidate and his running mate, however, may become untenable and harm their chances in November.

Presidential candidates often want a candidate who will add gravitas to his party's ticket, but will not upstage him. (When a vice presidential candidate is viewed as stronger than the presidential candidate, this is known as a "kangaroo ticket," because kangaroos use their hind legs for jumping.) A candidate without much foreign policy experience may look for a running mate who can fill that void. In 2000, Bush's choice of Cheney, a former Defense Secretary, offered experience in foreign affairs that Bush lacked. In 2008, Barack Obama was criticized for a lack of foreign policy experience. He chose as his running mate Delaware Senator Joe Biden, who was the chairman of the Senate Foreign Relations Committee.

A presumptive presidential nominee may also hope that his running mate can put in play states that would otherwise be out of reach. The ability, however, of vice presidential candidates to expand the electoral map for their party is highly questionable. When John Kerry chose Senator John Edwards as his vice presidential nominee, many Democrats hoped Edwards would help carry his home state of North Carolina for the Democrats in November. On Election Day, North Carolina went for Bush by a 12-point margin. In 1988, Democratic presidential nominee Michael Dukakis lost by a 13-point margin in Texas—the home state of his running mate, Senator Lloyd Benson.

Sometimes, a presidential candidate looks for a running mate who can add a bit of excitement and energy to a lethargic campaign. In 2008, John McCain had considerable difficulty inspiring the enthusiasm that characterized Obama's presence on the campaign trail. In a gamble, he chose Sarah Palin—the unknown and relatively inexperienced governor of Alaska—to be his running mate. To be sure, Palin energized conservative voters who had long viewed McCain warily. After a number of gaffes and a damaging performance in an interview with CBS's Katie Couric, however, she was widely seen as a drag on the Republican ticket.

While personal chemistry may play some role in choosing a running mate, this is rarely the decisive factor. Above all else, presidential candidates are looking for someone who can help them—in any way—reach the magic number of 270 electoral votes. In addition, they are looking for a viable successor; if tragedy strikes and the president is killed, the vice president takes over for his or her deceased predecessor.

The announcement of a running mate is done with considerable fanfare. Since presidential hopefuls generally make their choice for vice president official in the days leading up to the nominating convention, this marks the beginning of a weeklong whirlwind of political activity. Often, a presidential candidate's "short list" of running mates—the list of final contenders for the job—is leaked to the media. Reporters and pundits then spend countless hours speculating and pontificating about whom the presumptive nominee is most likely to choose. Once the presumptive nominee has finalized his choice, the name may be leaked to reporters a few hours before the official announcement is set to take place. Meeting with potential veep candidates, either secretly or with public fanfare, is a way to build interest and support among various groups and constituencies. For a politician, even getting mentioned as a possible contender is an honor.

For the big announcement, the campaign assembles a large crowd of supporters. The presidential candidate gives a brief speech introducing and lauding his choice for vice president. Then, the vice presidential candidate gives his or her own speech, introducing him or herself to the public. From that moment on, the two running mates campaign as a team—although not necessarily together. They do arrange for some joint appearances, but more often the presidential nominee will deploy his vice presidential running mate to areas where he or she is expected to help the ticket the most.

In 2008, Barack Obama sent his running mate, Joe Biden, to areas with working class and older voters in Pennsylvania, Ohio, and Florida—places where Obama had demonstrated political weakness during the primaries.[9] Biden (a native of Scranton, Pennsylvania, who had represented Delaware in the U.S. Senate for thirty years) frequently invoked his blue-collar roots on the campaign trail. While Obama was often described as cool, professorial, and even aloof in certain campaign settings, Biden was known for his informal style, lighthearted humor, and legendary loquaciousness.* He also assumed the traditional campaign role often assigned to vice presidential candidates: the attack dog. He continually lit in to John McCain, attacking him as "out of touch" with the economic concerns of average Americans.

Sometimes, vice presidential selections go awry. Pundits often describe George H. W. Bush's choice of Dan Quayle as a strategic blunder, given Quayle's tendency toward verbal gaffes. Others would point to 1984 Democratic nominee Walter Mondale's choice of Geraldine Ferraro, who was hounded by questions on the campaign trail about her husband's finances. Yet in both of these cases—and many, many others involving problematic vice presidential candidacies—the two running mates remained a team until the bitter end. Quayle went on to serve as vice president under Bush.

In 1972, however, one vice presidential candidate proved so controversial that he was forced off the ticket. Democratic presidential nominee George McGovern had chosen Thomas Eagleton, a liberal Democratic senator from Missouri, as his running mate. However, Eagleton's past treatment for depression—which included medication and electroshock therapy—posed a major problem for the McGovern/Eagleton ticket. After initially

---

* The *New York Times*'s Mark Leibovich wrote of Biden: "He is a distinctive blend of pit bull and odd duck whose weak filters make him capable of blurting out pretty much anything—'gaffes,' out-of-nowhere comments (pivoting mid-speech to say 'Excuse my back!' to people seated behind him), goofy asides (tapping a reporter's chest and telling him, 'You need to work on your pecs.')"[10]

backing Eagleton, McGovern asked him to withdraw. He replaced Eagleton with Sargent Shriver, a former ambassador and brother-in-law to John, Robert, and Ted Kennedy.

Clearly, the selection of a vice presidential running mate is one of the most important moments in the campaign. It marks the end of the primary season, and the kickoff of the nominating convention and general election. In choosing a running mate, a presidential candidate selects a partner, and often, a chief surrogate. While much of what happens throughout the course of a campaign is beyond a candidate's control (economic crises, events abroad, etc.), choosing a vice presidential candidate is one of the few major campaign developments that a candidate can control. Perhaps most importantly, candidates know that their choice for vice president is the heir to their administration and their legacy; if a president dies in office—as has happened eight times—the burden of governing falls to the vice president.

★ THE BALLOTING ★

In the past, political parties' nominating conventions were far less predictable affairs than they are today. The names of politicians who had not campaigned for the presidency at all could be placed in nomination. This mainly occurred in "brokered conventions," in which no candidate wins enough delegates to win the nomination.* In modern conventions, the names that will be placed in nomination—as well as the

---

* This scenario actually featured prominently in an episode of the hit TV series *The West Wing*. Eric Baker, the fictional Democratic Governor of Pennsylvania, tried to win his party's nomination from the convention floor despite having sat out the primaries.

eventual winner—are more or less a foregone conclusion. In 1960, John F. Kennedy was not assured of victory going into the first ballot, but he did prevail. The last truly brokered convention was 1952 when it took three ballots for Democrat Adlai Stevenson to secure the nomination.

At the convention, the delegates organize themselves by state. Thus, all of California's delegates are gathered in one area, Texas's in another, and so on.

Once the balloting begins, the convention's secretary conducts the roll call for each state, in alphabetical order. First, the secretary calls on Alabama. A spokesman for the Alabama delegation announces that Alabama casts 38 votes for (the fictional) Senator Thomas, 13 votes for Governor Magnuson, and 2 votes for Senator Brown. Alaska's delegation announces their state casts 10 votes for Thomas, 5 for Magnuson, and 3 for Brown, etc.

When the voting has concluded, the winner of a majority of delegates has officially been nominated for president. (However, this candidate will formally accept the nomination on the last day of the convention.) If no candidate receives a majority of delegates, the event becomes a "brokered convention." In brokered conventions, the candidates try to increase their share of delegates through deal making and bargaining. The state delegations then cast their votes on a second ballot, and third and fourth if need be. Essentially, the voting continues until a candidate has clinched the nomination. Brokered conventions, however, became exceedingly rare after states began holding primary elections; attempts by delegates to overturn the expressed will of the voters would create a politically untenable situation for a nominee and his or her political party. The term "smoke-filled room" was coined in 1920 to describe the process where party insiders, typically cigar-smoking party bosses, engineered the nomination after ten ballots of Warren Harding, who turned out to be one of the most corrupt and consistently low-rated presidents.

In 2008, the roll call at the Democratic National Convention was not quite business as usual. Although Senator Hillary Rodham Clinton had conceded the race for the Democratic nomination to Barack Obama in June, questions remained as to whether Obama could unite the Democratic Party. The Democratic presidential contest had been bitter at times, and some of Clinton's supporters were slow to warm to Obama.

When the convention's secretary recognized the Illinois delegation (Illinois, of course, was Obama's home state), it's spokesman yielded to New York (Clinton's home state). At that moment, Clinton made a dramatic entrance onto the convention floor and made her way to the microphone. She addressed the delegates and requested that the convention, in a demonstration of party unity, suspend the roll call and nominate Obama by acclamation:

> On behalf of the great state of New York, with appreciation for the spirit and dedication of all who are gathered here, with eyes firmly fixed on the future, in the spirit of unity, with the goal of victory, with faith in our party and country, let's declare together in one voice, right here and right now, that Barack Obama is our candidate and he will be our president. . . . I move that Senator Barack Obama of Illinois be selected by this convention by acclamation as the nominee of the Democratic Party for president of the United States.[11]

While Obama would certainly have been nominated without Clinton's gesture, her speech helped to unify the convention behind its Democratic nominee. Thus, Obama was able to pivot to the general election knowing that he had a united Democratic party behind him.

★ THE ACCEPTANCE SPEECH ★

On the last night of each party's national convention, the nominee formally accepts the nomination for president in an "acceptance speech." Those speeches generally include a variation on: "I accept your nomination for president of the United States of America!" In addition to formally accepting the title "nominee," candidates use acceptance speeches to define their candidacy for the general election.

Here are excerpts from past acceptance speeches at Democratic and Republican national conventions:

In 2008, Senator Barack Obama (D-IL) said: "We are more compassionate than a government that lets veterans sleep on our streets and families slide into poverty; that sits on its hands while a major American city drowns before our eyes. Tonight, I say to the American people, to Democrats and Republicans and Independents across this great land—enough! This moment—this election—is our chance to keep, in the 21st century, the American promise alive."[12]

That same year, Senator John McCain (R-AZ) told delegates to the Republican National Convention: "I hate war. It's terrible beyond imagination. I'm running for president to keep the country I love safe and prevent other families from risking their loved ones in war as my family has. I will draw on all my experience with the world and its leaders, and all the tools at our disposal—diplomatic, economic, military, and the power of our ideals—to build the foundations for a stable and enduring peace."

In 1992 Bill Clinton told delegates: "And so, in the name of all the people who do the work, pay the taxes, raise the kids and play by the rules, in the name of the hard-working Americans who make up our forgotten middle class, I accept your nomination for President of the United States. I am a product of that middle class. And when I am President you will be forgotten no more."[13]

In 1980, Ronald Reagan accepted the Republican nomination for president, telling delegates: "I will not accept the excuse that the federal government has grown so big and powerful that it is beyond the control of any President, any Administration, or Congress. We are going to put an end to the notion that the American taxpayer exists to fund the federal government. The federal government—The federal government exists to serve the American people. On January 20th, we are going to re-establish that truth."[14]

At the 1964 Democratic National Convention, President Lyndon B. Johnson laid out his vision of a great society: "This nation—this generation—in this hour, has man's first chance to build the Great Society—a place where the meaning of man's life matches the marvels of man's labor. We seek a nation where every man can find reward in work and satisfaction in the use of his talents. We seek a nation where every man can seek knowledge, and touch beauty, and rejoice in the closeness of family and community. We seek a nation where every man can, in the words of our oldest promise, follow the pursuit of happiness—not just security—but achievements and excellence and fulfillment of the spirit."[15]

In 1952, Republican delegates gathered in Chicago for their party's national convention. Their candidate, Dwight D. Eisenhower, said: "We are now at a moment in history when, under God, this nation of ours has become the mightiest temporal power and the mightiest spiritual force on earth. The destiny of mankind—the making of a world that will be fit for our children to live in—hangs in the balance on what we say and what we accomplish in these months ahead. We must use our power wisely for the good of all our people. If we do this, we will open a road into the future on which today's Americans, young and old, and the generations that come after them, can go forward—go forward to a life in which there will be far greater abundance of material, cultural, and spiritual rewards than our forefathers or we ever dreamed of."[16]

★ HOW THE PRIMARIES AND CONVENTIONS HAVE ★ EVOLVED: THE MCGOVERN-FRASER REFORMS

In April of 1968, Hubert Humphrey declared his candidacy for the presidency of the United States. Humphrey, the incumbent vice president and former U.S. senator from Minnesota, then went on to win the Democratic nomination without having competed in a single primary. In those days, not all states even held primary elections, and the powerful Democratic Party insiders played a far more influential role in nominating contests.

To be sure, 1968 saw a campaign for the Democratic nomination like no other. President Johnson decided not to seek a full second term. Robert F. Kennedy, a senator from New York and brother of the slain John F. Kennedy, was assassinated moments after a crucial victory in the California primary. After Johnson's exit and RFK's murder, the race for the Democratic nomination came down to two Minnesotans: Humphrey and the enigmatic hero to antiwar liberals, Senator Eugene McCarthy. McCarthy's opposition to the Vietnam War had fueled his rise from obscurity after he nearly upset President Johnson in the New Hampshire primary. (Johnson had not yet withdrawn from the race at that time).

Humphrey, fairly or not, was the heir to the LBJ legacy in the minds of many Democratic voters. Despite his long, distinguished record on the front lines of American liberalism—including an impassioned speech in favor of civil rights legislation at the 1948 Democratic National Convention—his association with Johnson and the Vietnam War dogged him throughout his campaign.

Yet in 1968, just over one third of convention delegates were chosen in primaries. In fact, only seventeen states even held primaries. The rest held state conventions, in which party leaders would choose delegates. These party leaders—often called "party bosses"—favored establishment candidates. Thus, it was no surprise that Humphrey—the incumbent vice president—won the support of the Democratic Party insiders who controlled nearly two thirds of the convention's delegates. Without having competed in a single primary, Humphrey won the Democratic nomination for president despite Democratic voters' clear preference for Bobby Kennedy and Gene McCarthy.

The party bosses had ignored the Democratic electorate. And they paid for it. Having failed to unite a bitterly divided Democratic Party, Humphrey lost the 1968 presidential election to Richard M. Nixon. Perhaps more importantly, a successful reform effort by two Midwestern, liberal Democrats would soon strip the party elites of the power to rig the presidential nominating process.[17]

Following the 1968 presidential election, South Dakota Senator George McGovern and Minnesota Representative Donald Fraser chaired a commission charged with making the nominating process less corrupt and more democratic. The commission sharply limited the ability of state party leaders to choose delegates, and required that women, young voters, and minority groups be represented in state delegations in numbers that were proportional to their populations. The effect of these rules was profound and nearly immediate. For example, women accounted for 40 percent of delegates at the 1972 Democratic National Convention, compared to just 13 percent in 1968.

One of the clear beneficiaries of the McGovern-Fraser reforms was . . . George McGovern. McGovern stepped down as chairman of the commission in 1971 in order to run for president the following year. The commission's requirements that women, minorities, and young voters be better represented among delegates were clearly a boon to McGovern, who enjoyed strong support from college students and the party's liberal base. In 1972, he accomplished what McCarthy could not. He won the Democratic nomination for president. (McGovern, however, was far less successful in the general election: He suffered one of the greatest landslide defeats in American history, capturing only 37 percent of the popular vote and carrying only Massachusetts and the District of Columbia.)

The McGovern-Fraser Commission technically only overhauled the rules governing the *Democratic* nominating process. Republicans, however, adopted similar rules for their nominating conventions. Thus, the McGovern-Fraser reforms had a lasting, powerful impact on presidential elections.

★ THE HUNT COMMISSION: A REACTION TO ★ McGOVERN-FRASER

Some in the Democratic Party felt that the McGovern-Fraser reforms made the Democratic nominating process *too democratic*. The Democrats suffered landslide electoral defeats both in 1972 (when McGovern himself won the nomination) and in 1980, when Carter lost his reelection bid. In 1982, in order to temper the effects of McGovern-Fraser, a commission led by North Carolina Governor Jim Hunt restored some power enjoyed by Democratic elites.

The Hunt commission established "superdelegates," which were discussed previously. The Democrats who implemented these changes believed that granting delegate status to those with an abiding interest in the long-term success of the party (Democratic governors, members of Congress, etc.) would prevent another nomination that yielded disastrous results on Election Day.[18] Still, critics argued that superdelegates allowed Democratic insiders to overturn the will of the voters, and thus created an inherently undemocratic nominating system.

CHAPTER

☆ **4** ☆

THE GENERAL
ELECTION

★ THE ELECTORAL COLLEGE ★

I f U.S. presidents were elected by a popular vote—meaning that the candidate with the most votes cast throughout the entire country wins—then the general election campaign would look quite different. The Democratic candidate might campaign heavily in New York City to run up his or her margins in that urban bastion of Democratic liberalism. Or the Republican might campaign heavily in Texas, the most populous Republican-leaning state in the country.

Yet presidents are not elected by the popular vote, but rather by the *Electoral College*. In the Electoral College, each state is represented by a number of electors that is equal to its number of senators plus its number of House members. For example, New York had twenty-nine members of the House of Representatives in 2008. All states are represented by two senators. With twenty-nine House members and two senators, New York controlled thirty-one votes in the Electoral College in the 2008 presidential election. Vermont, meanwhile, is a small, sparsely populated state. It has only one member of the House of Representatives. With one House member and two senators, Vermont casts three electoral votes in the Electoral College.

In total, the Electoral College is made up of 538 electors or electoral votes. The winner of the presidential election must win a majority of electoral votes—270, to be exact. States' electoral votes are adjusted every ten years after the census releases data on population growth in every state.

Each state's population determines its number of seats in the House of Representatives, and thus affects its total allocation of electoral votes. Following the 2010 Census, New York lost two seats due to slow population growth.[1] Texas, meanwhile, gained four House seats and thus four electoral votes as a result of strong population growth.[2]

ELECTORAL VOTE DISTRIBUTION

According to the 2010 Census, the Electoral College's 538 electoral votes will be distributed as follows:[3]

Alabama	9	Kansas	6
Alaska	3	Kentucky	8
Arizona	11	Louisiana	8
Arkansas	6	Maine	4
California	55	Maryland	10
Colorado	9	Massachusetts	11
Connecticut	7	Michigan	16
Delaware	3	Minnesota	10
Florida	29	Mississippi	6
Georgia	16	Missouri	10
Hawaii	4	Montana	3
Idaho	4	Nebraska	5
Illinois	20	Nevada	6
Indiana	11	New Hampshire	4
Iowa	6	New Jersey	14

New Mexico	5	Tennessee	11
New York	29	Texas	38
North Carolina	15	Utah	6
North Dakota	3	Vermont	3
Ohio	18	Virginia	13
Oklahoma	7	Washington	12
Oregon	7	West Virginia	5
Pennsylvania	20	Wisconsin	10
Rhode Island	4	Wyoming	3
South Carolina	9	District of Columbia	3
South Dakota	3		

Since 538 is an even number, a tie in the electoral college (269–269) is possible. If no candidate receives a majority of electoral votes, the House of Representatives chooses the president, while the U.S. Senate selects the vice president. (This has been true since the ratification of the Twelfth Amendment to the constitution in 1804.)

If the election is thrown in to the House of Representatives, each state delegation casts one vote. Thus, California, New York, and Texas would have equal voting power to Vermont, New Hampshire, and Idaho. In other words, if the Democratic candidate receives a majority of votes from California's House members, the California delegations casts one vote in favor of the Democratic candidate. Thus, even if one party controls a majority of seats in the House, this does not guarantee that its presidential candidate would prevail if the House were to decide the presidential election. *Rather, the party must control a majority of state delegations in the House.*

This constitutional contingency plan could produce a divided executive branch of the federal government. For example, if the Republican Party controlled a majority of state delegations in the House of Representatives, it would presumably elect a Republican president. But if the Democrats controlled the Senate, that chamber would likely elect a Democratic vice president. In this scenario, the country could conceivably be governed by a president and vice president from opposing political parties.

While a tie in the Electoral College is theoretically possible in every presidential election, the chances of such a scenario actually unfolding are remote. In fact, the last tie occurred in 1800. In that election, Thomas Jefferson and Aaron Burr—who was Jefferson's preferred vice presidential candidate—both received 73 electoral votes. The House eventually elected Jefferson as president.

The House of Representatives again chose the president in 1824. That year, Andrew Jackson won the popular vote, but failed to win a majority in the Electoral College. John Quincy Adams, the son of former President John Adams, came in second in the popular vote behind Jackson. The House of Representatives elected Adams as president. Like his father, the younger Adams served a single term: He was defeated by Jackson in a rematch in 1828.

It should be noted that the Electoral College does not actually convene as a body following presidential elections. Rather electors meet at their state capitals in December (specifically, the first Monday after the second Wednesday in December) to cast votes for the presidential and vice presidential candidates who won their home states. The gap between Election Day and the meeting of the Electoral College was originally intended to give electors sufficient time to travel from their homes to state capitals; after all, the Electoral College was conceived in the eighteenth century, and was subject to the limitations of eighteenth century travel.

WHO ARE ELECTORS AND WHERE DO THEY COME FROM?

Electors are the people who actually vote in the Electoral College. Under the U.S. Constitution, states have the authority to appoint electors. In some states, they are nominated in the same primaries that choose presidential nominees. Other states nominate electors at state party conventions. The Constitution bars all federal office holders from serving as electors. (This includes members of both houses of Congress, as well as officeholders who are appointed by the president.)

While all of this may seem dull, archaic, and purely technical, the Electoral College profoundly shapes the nature of presidential campaigns. More specifically, the winner-take-all nature of the Electoral College* can produce lopsided victories that in no way reflect the popular vote.

For example, if one candidate wins California by a 51–49 percent margin, that candidate receives all 55 of California's electoral

---

* Maine and Nebraska are exceptions—those states award partially their electoral votes by congressional district. (For representation in the House of Representatives, each state is broken into different congressional districts. One House member represents each of those districts.) For example, Maine has two congressional districts (which also means it is represented by two members of the House of Representatives) and four electoral votes (2 House members + 2 senators = 4 electoral votes). It awards two of its electoral votes to the statewide winner. The other two are allocated according to who wins each congressional district. If Candidate A loses the statewide popular vote in Maine but manages to win the popular vote in one of its congressional districts, that candidate would still win one electoral vote. The other candidate— the winner of the statewide vote and the other congressional district—would receive three electoral votes.

votes. One oddity of the Electoral College—some would argue it is a serious flaw—is the possibility of a candidate winning the presidency while losing the popular vote. This happened most recently in the 2000 presidential election, in which Vice President Al Gore received the most votes, but then-Texas Governor George W. Bush won in the Electoral College after narrowly being declared the winner in Florida. (More on this later.) The presidential elections of 1876 and 1888 also produced victors who lost the popular vote, albeit by small margins. In 1876, Samuel J. Tilden won the popular vote but lost in the Electoral College to Rutherford B. Hayes. In 1888, Benjamin Harrison was elected president despite losing the popular vote to Grover Cleveland.

Another practical effect of electing a president through Electoral College is a campaign that is not truly national in scope. During the general election, presidential candidates rarely visit states they seem certain to win. A Democrat who wins New York will receive all 29 electoral votes regardless of whether he or she wins 51 or 80 percent of the statewide popular vote. And since a Democrat is heavily favored to win New York during presidential elections, no Democrat would waste precious time and resources in the Empire State. Conversely, no Republican presidential candidate would campaign in New York; no matter how close the margin of victory, the loser is awarded nothing.

Thus, presidential candidates spend little if any time in states such as New York, California, Massachusetts, New Jersey, or Maryland (all of which are currently leaning heavily toward Democrats at the statewide level). Similarly, Texas, Alabama, Mississippi, Oklahoma, and Kansas—all of which have a distinct Republican lean—see very little in the way of visits from presidential candidates.

So Where Do Candidates Spend Their Time?

For the most part, presidential nominees campaign in "swing states," or "battleground states." These states are highly competitive in presidential contests, and do not show a strong preference for either party from one election to the next. In the battleground states, candidates flood the airwaves with political advertisements, hold rallies, and try to energize their hard-core supporters while being careful not to alienate undecided voters.

Ohio, Florida, Pennsylvania, Missouri, Michigan, and Wisconsin are all good examples of swing states. However, these battlegrounds shift over time. West Virginia, for example, was once a swing state but has shown little interest in Democratic presidential candidates as of late. Colorado and Virginia were long regarded as "Republican states," but are now highly competitive battlegrounds and were both won by Barack Obama in 2008.

Some swing states "swing" more than others. Missouri's electorate is closely divided between Democrats and Republicans and is often referred to as a swing state. Yet it has voted Republican for president in 2000, 2004, and 2008—albeit by a razor-thin margin in the last 2008 election.

Michigan and Minnesota are both politically competitive states and receive many visits from presidential hopefuls. Yet Minnesota has not voted for a Republican presidential candidate since 1972. Michigan last voted for the GOP at the presidential level in 1988.

Ohio has voted for the winner of every presidential election since 1964. Florida, meanwhile, is home to some of the most closely divided elections in the country—and presidential elections are no exception. Since 2000, it has been one of the most bitterly contested states in the country.

THE 2000 ELECTION DEBACLE & BUSH VS. GORE

The 2000 presidential election was one of the closest in American history. Nationally, Democrat Al Gore received 48.4 percent of the popular vote to Republican George W. Bush's 47.9 percent. Green Party candidate Ralph Nader took 2.7 percent of the vote nationally. But in U.S. presidential elections, the Electoral College is what matters. And Election Night in 2000 produced an Electoral College divide so stark that the entire election came down to the result in Florida, where the two candidates were locked in a virtual tie.

At 8 p.m., all of the major television networks declared Gore the winner in Florida. At that moment, it looked as though the election was all but over. Michigan—a highly competitive state that was bitterly contested in 2000—was also called for Gore. Shortly before 9 p.m., Gore added Pennsylvania to his column. Having won these three critical states, the networks had all but declared him the president-elect.

Then, confusion took hold. Shortly before 10 p.m., viewers saw 25 electoral votes disappear from Gore's Electoral Vote tally on the television screen. In an unprecedented turn of events, the networks retracted its earlier call of Florida for Gore. What happened? The *exit polls* were wrong.

★ WHAT ARE EXIT POLLS? ★

Exit polls are surveys of voters taken after they have left the voting booth. Voters are asked which candidates they voted for, in addition to personal demographic information (race, income, etc.). Using statistical sampling, exit polls are employed to make projections as to which candidate prevailed in each state. On Election Night in 2000, exit polling showed Al Gore defeating George W. Bush in Florida. This was viewed as a deathblow to the Bush camp, which had counted on the Sunshine State being part of the GOP coalition. Most political observers assumed Florida was Bush country—after all, Bush's brother, Jeb Bush, was the current governor of that state at the time. Thus, Gore's projected victory was considered something of an upset.

As viewers soon found out, exit polling is an inexact science. And in 2000, they failed in spectacular fashion. After the initial call of Florida for Gore, the *actual votes* trickled in. And the vote totals showed a very different pattern than the exit polls. Thus, the networks retracted their Florida projection.

At 2:17 a.m., the networks called Florida for Bush, and with it, the presidency. Gore called Bush to concede the election.

★ THEN IT HAPPENED AGAIN. ★

Shortly before 4 a.m., it became clear that heavily Democratic precincts in Florida were delivering for Al Gore. Bush's lead in the statewide vote tally began to shrink, and then all but vanished. With the two candidates separated by less than 2,000 votes, the networks once again retracted their call of Florida for Bush. By this time, it had become clear that the winner in Florida would win the election. Thus, all networks also retracted their earlier declaration that Bush had won the presidency.

With such a small margin separating Gore and Bush, Florida state law required a statewide machine recount of all votes cast in the election. When that recount had concluded, Bush led by just 327 votes.

By this time, both the Gore and Bush camps had assembled legal teams. Gore's lawyers sought a manual recount in four counties where they believed ballots cast by Democratic voters had been wrongly discarded. (Specifically, Gore requested a manual recount in these counties: Miami-Dade, Broward, Palm Beach, and Volusia.) Gore supporters maintained that voting irregularities warranted a recount in those areas. Critics argued that Gore was simply trying to net more votes out of four Democratic counties. Gore's legal efforts centered on ballots in which a vote for president had not been properly indicated.

On each ballot, there was a hole corresponding to a candidate's name. In order to vote for a candidate, the voter was required to punch the hole completely. Yet in some cases, the hole corresponding to Gore's name had been dented (these votes came to be known as "dimpled chads") or punctured, but not completely removed ("hanging chads"). These ballots were known as "undervotes." (Ballots in which voters punched holes for more than one presidential candidate were known as "overvotes.")

Ballots with dimpled and hanging chads had been discounted as the votes were tabulated. Gore supporters argued that such ballots should be counted where the intent of the voter was clear. Bush's team argued that a standard that interpreted voter intent was too subjective, and thus could not be administered fairly.

Over the next week—November 11 through November 17—those four counties began to carry out the hand recounts requested by Gore. Bush's lawyers sued to halt the counting. On November 13, a federal court refused to stop the manual recount, a decision welcomed by the Gore campaign.

Throughout this legal process, there were other political machinations going on. Florida's chief election official, Secretary of State Katherine Harris, refused requests to include manually recounted ballots in the official statewide tally. Harris, however, was not merely Florida's chief election official. She was also the chairperson of Bush's presidential campaign in Florida. Many Democrats argued that this represented an inherent conflict of interest, and that she was acting as a political operative attempting to rig the result for her preferred candidate.

On November 20, Gore lawyers argued before the Florida Supreme Court that the manually recounted ballots should be included in the official certified total. The next day, the state's high court sided with Gore. However, the court also allowed Florida election officials to certify the statewide vote on November 26. Miami-Dade County subsequently cancelled its manual recount, contending that it was impossible to complete its count by that date.

Bush's lawyers opposed allowing manual ballots to be counted in the statewide total, and appealed the Florida Supreme Court's decision to the U.S. Supreme Court. They contended that Florida law did not allow for manual recounts, and that the Florida Supreme Court had rewritten state election law after the vote had taken place. The U.S. Supreme Court agreed to hear the case, and announced that proceedings would begin on December 1.

However, the issue of whether manually counted ballots should be counted was temporarily put on hold when Katherine Harris certified Bush as the official winner on November 26. Gore immediately sued to challenge the official vote tally. At this point, Bush's official lead in Florida was 537 votes.

On December 4, the U.S. Supreme Court reversed the Florida Supreme Court decision requiring manually recounted ballots to be included in the official total. In addition, the high court sent the case back to the Florida Supreme Court with instructions to clarify its earlier ruling. A Florida circuit court also ruled against Gore's effort to overturn the state's November 26 certification of a Bush victory. Both decisions were major setbacks for the Gore campaign.

Gore then appealed the circuit court ruling to the Florida Supreme Court, where the Gore and Bush campaign lawyers faced off once more. On December 8, Florida's Supreme Court reversed the circuit court ruling and ordered a statewide recount of all "undervotes." Bush appealed this decision, and the case reached the U.S. Supreme Court the following day.

The court ordered that all manual recounts cease immediately and heard arguments from both the Bush and Gore camps. On December 11, the U.S. Supreme Court overturned the Florida Supreme Court's ruling, which effectively ended the legal dispute and ensured that Bush would win Florida, and thus the presidency. The 5–4 split decision in Bush v Gore remains controversial because the nine justices did not speak with one voice, opening themselves up to the charge that they reached the decision on political grounds rather than sound judicial reasoning.

The Florida state legislature also posed a formidable obstacle to Gore's efforts to claim the state's 25 electoral votes. While legal proceedings were still going on, the Florida state House of Representatives planned a special legislative session to choose 25 electors all pledged to Bush. (And the state House eventually did precisely that on December 12.) Thus, while the Gore campaign hoped to prevail in court, it all may have been for naught.

Even if the courts had allowed for recounts that enabled Gore to eek out a narrow victory, he likely would have been thwarted by the Florida state legislature and its handpicked slate of electors loyal to Bush.

On December 13—more than one month after Election Day—Gore conceded defeat and gave a televised speech in which he called for national reconciliation. And thus ended the disputed election of 2000, in which George W. Bush won the presidency despite losing the popular vote. His official margin of victory in Florida was 537 votes. In percentage terms, he defeated Gore in the Sunshine State by a margin of 48.847 percent–48.838 percent.[4,5]

★ ANOTHER BUNGLED ELECTORAL PROJECTION: ★ DEWEY DEFEATS TRUMAN

The 2000 election was not the first time that election projections turned out to be wrong. Following the 1948 presidential election, President Harry S. Truman posed for a photograph as he held up the front page of the *Chicago Tribune*. The paper's lead headline read: "Dewey Defeats Truman." Despite his reported loss to New York Governor Thomas Dewey, Truman is smiling widely in the photograph. Why? Because Dewey had not defeated Truman at all. In fact, Truman had been elected with 303 electoral votes to Dewey's 189. Making matters worse for the paper, it had also predicted Republican control of both houses of Congress. In fact, Democrats had regained control of both the House and the Senate.

In fairness to the *Chicago Tribune*, the paper did not have at its disposal the sophisticated resources for predicting elections that news outlets use today. And its prediction was perfectly in line with what was thought to be a foregone conclusion leading up to Election Day in 1948. News outlets and columnists and even public opinion polling had predicted a sweeping Dewey victory.

In addition, Truman had been fighting off not only his Republican challenger, but two other candidates with strong ties to Democratic constituencies. South Carolina Governor Strom Thurmond, running as a southern, prosegregation "Dixiecrat," threatened to siphon votes from what had become known as the "solid South"—the Democrat's loyal southern base. (Indeed, Thurmond carried South Carolina, Mississippi, Alabama, and Louisiana.) Yet Truman also faced a challenge from the liberal wing of the Democratic Party in the form of Henry Wallace, a staunch liberal who served as vice president under FDR from 1941 to 1945 and ran against Truman under the Progressive Party banner.[6,7] Truman overcame the three-way split in his party with an aggressive campaign against the overly confident Dewey and the "do-nothing" Congress controlled by Republicans. Truman's blistering attacks won him the moniker, "Give 'em hell Harry." On Election night, the president went to bed, awakening at 4 a.m. to learn from a radio report that he was almost two million votes ahead. He had edged out Dewey in the key states of Ohio, California, and Illinois, capitalizing on a recovering economy and his claim that economic hard times could return under Republican leadership. Wallace's Progressives took fewer votes than expected from the Democrats' liberal base, receiving only 2.4 percent of the vote.

★ THE RACE FOR THE WHITE HOUSE: ★ A NATIONAL, STATE, AND LOCAL CAMPAIGN

By nature, presidential campaigns are national in scope. They turn mostly on national issues, rather than provincial concerns that affect only one region of the country. Not surprisingly, presidential campaigns have national headquarters and a national campaign manager.

A presidential candidate's national headquarters is often but not always located in his or her home state. If the governor of Michigan were to run for president, that state would most likely serve as the campaign's home base. When a president is running for reelection, he often chooses Washington DC as the location for his campaign headquarters. A president, regardless of whether he or she once served a governor or senator, now represents the entire country and has a national constituency. Thus, DC perhaps makes sense in this regard. President Obama, counter to the recent trend and sensitive to the antigovernment mood in the country, centered his 2012 reelection campaign in Chicago.

The campaign manager is the person who is most in charge of "running the campaign." Generally, all other staffers report to this person. If a campaign is floundering, its manager is often ultimately held responsible—and fired. Other important staff members at the national level include a communications director who coordinates national messaging for the campaign, as well as a finance director who is charged with coordinating the campaign's fundraising operation.

In addition to a campaign manager, presidential campaigns will also sometimes hire a "chief strategist." Under this staffing structure, the campaign manager assumes day-to-day supervisory and managerial duties, while the strategist fulfills more of a "big picture" role.

As presidential campaigns have evolved over time, so too have their staff. All campaigns have media specialists to oversee their advertising. These ads, generally speaking, praise the candidate and attack his or her opponent. In the last decade, presidential campaigns began hiring "new media" specialists who perform yet another distinct role. Recognizing the growing political importance of blogs and Internet-based communities, presidential campaigns responded by hiring individuals to facilitate outreach to those communities.

While presidential campaigns are national in scope and structure, they also entail state-based operations. Campaigns appoint state chairmen and or "state directors." These chairmen can be elected officials—members of Congress, governors, or other state-wide officeholders—or professional political operatives. In addition, state party chairmen are working hard to deliver votes for their presidential nominee. They are also busy, however, trying to win Senate and House seats, as well as governorships and seats in the state legislatures.

Presidential campaigns are perhaps most visible to average voters at the local level. All over the country—and particularly in politically competitive states (the "swing states"), campaigns open local headquarters on Main Street. In counties and towns that split evenly between Democrats and Republicans, the local operation uses an army of volunteers to reach undecided voters. In areas where a party usually performs well at the presidential level, volunteers strive to make sure their supporters are fired up and will show up in force at the polls on Election Day.

Local volunteers are the backbone of any presidential campaign, and they perform a variety of functions. Working out of field offices, they make phone calls to voters who are believed to be supporters of their candidate, and do everything possible to make sure they show up on Election Day. This is called "phone banking."

Volunteers hit the streets to greet voters face to face. They hand out campaign literature at train stations and parking lots of major shopping centers. They also knock on doors of local residents—and often have those same doors slammed in their faces. This is known as "canvassing," and it can be one of the most thankless—but also most important—activities involved in a successful presidential campaign.

Local volunteers carry their candidate's message directly to the voters, and often face the brunt of the public's dissatisfaction with the state of the campaign, and the direction of the country generally. Because canvassing can be grueling work, and is usually done for no pay, the "true believers" usually fill this role. Campaign volunteers are often—but not always—tried and true Democratic or Republican voters. They demonstrate a level of commitment to their political party or candidate that is stronger than the average voter.

At the local level, campaign workers also work in coordination with the state and national campaign organizations to organize events and plan venues for their candidates to give speeches, shake hands, and appear on local news programs.

Outside Groups

Independent groups have played an increasingly important role in presidential elections over the last decade. While outside political organizations (such as labor unions, business groups, and gun rights organizations) have been important actors in electoral battles for decades, they arguably took on a greater prominence and importance after 2002—when a major campaign finance reform law imposed stricter limits on campaign spending. In 2004, outside groups stepped in to fill the void, pouring money into the race between President George W. Bush and Senator John Kerry. MoveOn.org, a liberal organization that was fiercely opposed to Bush's policy agenda, allied itself with Kerry's campaign and took to the airwaves to attack the incumbent president.

Kerry, meanwhile, faced attacks from an outside group that proved to be devastating to his campaign. The "Swift Boat Veterans for Truth" ran television ads making the explosive allegation that Kerry had lied about his military record—specifically his service in the Vietnam War.

Kerry had made his Vietnam service a central theme in his campaign, and these attacks threatened to wound him with what was perceived to be his greatest political strength. While none of the Swift Boat attacks were found to have been factually accurate—and were debunked by numerous news organizations[8]—they proved politically potent. Perhaps most remarkably, the most devastating political ad of the 2004 election cycle was not run by a candidate's campaign—but by an outside group. Kerry accused the group of being a "front for the Bush campaign," but the Bush campaign denied the charge. While the group did not have any ties to the 2004 Bush campaign, they did have ties to Bush's closest political adviser, Karl Rove.

It should be noted that these outside groups—known by their tax label as "527s"—are legally barred from coordinating their activities with candidates' campaigns. In other words, they may share a political objective (electing a candidate), but they cannot legally maintain a collaborative relationship with a campaign. Of course, accusations of such collaboration run rampant as elections heat up. While the Kerry campaign accused the Swift Boat Veterans of coordinating campaign activities with the Bush campaign[9], the Bush team contended that Kerry's campaign had collaborated with liberal groups, including MoveOn .org, and Americans Coming Together.[10]

THE AIR WAR

While volunteers are the army that makes up a campaign's "ground game," modern presidential campaigns are waged in large part on television. Broadly speaking, there are two types of political ads: positive and negative. In positive political ads, candidates boast about their accomplishments and character, and try to come across as someone to whom voters can easily relate. These ads may include information about their voting records ("Senator Johnson voted to improve schools and fight crime . . .") or autobiographical information ("Governor Smith served this country as a soldier, created hundreds of jobs as a small business owner, and fought corruption as Governor . . ."). In these ads, candidates do everything possible to cast themselves in a positive light. They might speak directly into the camera from their front porch or backyard, surrounded by their spouse, young children, and even the family dog. They strive to come across to voters as likeable and accomplished.

Negative ads, by contrast, focus on a candidate's opponent. These commercials, not surprisingly, are meant to make one's opponent appear incompetent, corrupt, out-of-touch, nasty, and generally in favor of all kinds of dreadful things. Such ads might feature an unflattering or even doctored photo of a political opponent, or use grainy black-and-white footage to make their actions appear ominous. Such ads can be relatively mild ("Senator Thomas voted fifty-seven times to raise your taxes . . . ") or downright vicious ("Senator Thomas voted to put murderers, rapists, and child molesters back on the street . . ."). Are such ads accurate? It depends. They can be fully accurate, technically accurate but misleading, partly true, or demonstrably false. The campaign behind the ad will claim the ad was accurate. The target of the ad will claim it was a "smear"—a false, even defamatory ad.

Both candidates will always claim that they are running a largely positive campaign, while their opponent is running a relentlessly negative one. In reality, most campaigns use a mixture of positive and negative advertising.

Do Negative Ads Work?

Certainly they do. Otherwise, campaigns would surely not spend millions of dollars creating and airing them. While voters claim to dislike negative advertising, they are clearly swayed by them. In August, 2008, Mark Penn, a long-time strategist for Bill and Hillary Clinton (and who became something of a lightening rod during the Clinton/Obama primary campaign) wrote in Politico: "Clever negative advertising works. That is reality. The tactic meets with media and pundit disapproval and spawns accusations of negativity, but the reality is that a clever negative ad can be devastatingly effective."[11]

An effective negative ad need not be accurate. In order to be effective, it simply must force its target to respond to its charge. A candidate who spends most of his time on the campaign stump responding to his opponent's attacks is, by definition, "off-message." Rather than sticking to his favored script, he now spends most of his time responding to an opponent's attacks.

Thus, a candidate who is the target of a negative ad often responds with a *counterattack* rather than a simple defense of his record. Often, a campaign can descend into a never-ending back-and-forth of negative attacks in which each candidate tries to throw the other off his or her game.

★ OTHER WAYS OF REACHING THE VOTERS ★

Television is the predominant medium in which presidential candidates communicate with voters, but it is not the only one. Presidential hopefuls also run advertisements on radio that bombard voters during their morning and afternoon commutes. In addition, campaigns blast out e-mails to their supporters and craft advertisements that appear exclusively on the Internet. Campaigns also use "direct mail," in which they send voters pamphlets that make the case for their candidate and slam their opponents.

Newspaper and magazine endorsements used to feature more prominently in presidential elections than they do today. While campaigns will still communicate with editorial boards and welcome their endorsement, it remains unclear whether they sway a significant percentage of the electorate.

Of course, candidates give many, many speeches. At times, they draw large crowds and significant media attention. Generally, every candidate has a standard "stump speech" that he or she uses during the general election campaign. This speech is repeated at daily campaign events, and addresses the major themes and issues that are central to the candidate's campaign.

These speeches, it should be noted, are anything but spontaneous events. They are carefully planned, and designed by campaigns to make their candidate appear impressive and popular. Before a candidate is scheduled to give a speech at a given location, that candidate's "advance team" is dispatched to the location to make preparations. They fill the audience with voters who are loyal to the candidate, and distribute signs and buttons. All of this is intended to make it look as though the candidate has a strong, enthusiastic following. The advance team may even go so far as to ensure that voters who are friendly to their candidate ask easy, "softball" questions during a question-and-answer period that may follow a speech.

Of course, even the most carefully planned campaign event leaves open the possibility of unscripted moments. Sometimes, supporters of an opposing candidate will show up to a rally and heckle the person giving a speech. They may ask uncomfortable or embarrassing questions. Political activists who are not loyal to any one candidate, but rather to a cause, may show up in an effort to disrupt the event and force the candidate to address their issue. Sometimes, candidates simply misspeak, and say something politically unwise. After all, presidential candidates campaign for fourteen hours a day for the better part of eighteen months. They give hundreds of speeches. They are human, and at some point are bound to slip up. And when they do, their opponents want to be ready. Thus, many campaigns employ "trackers" to record their opponents' public events on camera.

Trackers literally follow candidates around with handheld camcorders in case they say something that could be used against them. One of the most famous incidents involving a tracker ended a presidential campaign before it even began. In 2006, Virginia Senator George Allen was widely known to hold presidential ambitions. He began visiting Iowa, the home of the first caucus during the primary season, and raising money for a national campaign. But there was one small obstacle: Before running for president in 2008, he needed to win reelection to the U.S. Senate in 2006.

Although he was widely viewed as the favorite, his campaign imploded following an incident in which he insulted a tracker employed by his Democratic opponent, former Secretary of the Navy James Webb. During a campaign speech, Allen turned to Webb's tracker, S. R. Siddarth, a University of Virginia student who was of Indian descent. Allen began to mock him, calling him "macaca"—a racial slur—and saying, "Welcome to America, and the real world of Virginia."

Allen claimed he had not known what "macaca" meant, and had made up the word on the spot. But the damage was done. Not only did the incident take Allen out of the running for the Republican presidential nomination—he lost his bid for reelection to the U.S. Senate to Webb in a major political upset.[12]

★ CAMPAIGN TACTICS: ★
MERELY MACHIAVELLIAN VS. ILLEGAL

Campaigns are filled with dirty tricks. Some are so common that they fail to even raise eyebrows. Sometimes, however, cynical political machinations cross not only an ethical line, but a legal one. The most egregious and shocking example of such a case involved President Richard M. Nixon, who was elected president in 1968 and reelected in 1972. The incident began when five men working for Nixon's reelection campaign burglarized the headquarters of the Democratic National Committee. Nixon was personally implicated in efforts to cover up the burglary and impede the ensuing investigation. Facing impeachment and removal from office, Nixon resigned as president on August 9, 1974. While many hoped that Nixon's resignation would help the nation to heal from a traumatizing political scandal, it spawned a public distrust and cynicism toward government from which the country has arguably never recovered.

Of course, campaigns often accuse their opponents of such dirty tricks when things go wrong. Just days before the 2000 presidential election, George W. Bush was confronted with news reports that he had been arrested in 1976 in Kennebunkport, Maine, for driving under the influence of alcohol. Bush supporters contended that Al Gore's campaign was behind the leak—although they had no proof to substantiate such an allegation. In his memoir, Bush campaign strategist Karl Rove wrote that he suspected (again, without offering proof) Gore's press secretary, Chris Lehane, was behind the DUI leak.[13]

★ REACHING THE VOTERS WITH ★ SPEECHES: A COLLECTION OF SOUND BITES

Very few voters will ever view or listen to an entire campaign speech. Indeed, they are far more likely to see snippets of such speeches on their local news. Thus, they view what TV editors choose to show them. As a result, candidates' speeches are often written to emphasize "sound bites"—pithy statements designed to grab headlines and perhaps an appearance on news programs. Such sound bites might be a searing attack on an opponent, a glib one-liner, or a brief statement encapsulating the central message of a candidate's campaign.

FAMOUS PRESIDENTIAL SOUND BITES

A number of presidential sound bites have stood the test of time and history.

When speaking to a nation ravaged by the Great Depression, FDR famously declared in his first inaugural address:

"So, first of all, let me assert my firm belief that the only thing we have to fear . . . is fear itself."

At his inauguration in 1961, President John F. Kennedy told the country: "Ask not what your country can do for you—ask what you can do for your country."

In 1987, President Ronald Regan gave a speech at Brandenberg Gate—near the Berlin Wall—in which he directly addressed Soviet leader Mikhail Gorbachev, saying "General Secretary Gorbachev, if you seek peace, if you seek prosperity for the Soviet Union and eastern Europe, if you seek liberalization, come here to this gate. Mr. Gorbachev, open this gate. Mr. Gorbachev, Mr. Gorbachev, tear down this wall!" In this case, the sound bite became: ". . . Mr. Gorbachev, tear down this wall!"[14]

Some sound bites can also come back to haunt candidates. In his speech to the 1988 Republican national convention, then-Vice President George H. W. Bush promised: "Read my lips: no new taxes." That pledge may have served him well in the 1988 general election campaign; he defeated Democratic nominee and Massachusetts Governor Michael Dukakis by a 7-point margin in the national popular vote, and won an Electoral College landslide.[15] However, Bush violated that pledge after signing legislation raising taxes in an effort to reduce the federal budget deficit. He had broken a central promise of his campaign, and he would pay dearly for it. The *New York Post* mocked the president in its headline that read: "Read My Lips: I Lied." Bush was overwhelmingly defeated for reelection in 1992.

★ PHOTO OPS ★

When candidates make public appearances at factories, local diners, and state fairs, they appear to be seeking the votes of the people whose hands they shake. In reality, these appearances are "photo opportunities," or "photo ops," in which the image of a candidate interacting with voters is staged for the cameras. So when you see a candidate shaking hands with someone at a local coffee shop, you are as much the target as the voter pictured in the newspaper or on the local news.

Campaign stops in which a candidate seeks face time with actual voters, as opposed to playing to the cameras, is known as "retail campaigning." In smaller and or less populated states, retail campaigning can prove effective. New Hampshire, for example, is a state known for its tradition of retail campaigning.

In large states with densely populated urban and suburban areas, however, such campaigning is unrealistic. For example, a candidate campaigning in Philadelphia or the surrounding suburbs, Cleveland, or Milwaukee cannot hope to meet all the residents in that city. Thus, presidential campaigns—which focus on winning larger, vote-rich states—have little use for retail campaigning. National campaigns are waged on the air—through ad campaigns, televised speeches, etc.

Like sound bites, photo ops can backfire. One of the most famous photo ops gone awry dogged Michael Dukakis during his presidential campaign against George H. W. Bush. In an effort to combat attacks that he was "soft" on national security, Dukakis visited a General Dynamics (a defense contractor) plant in Michigan, and went for a ride in a tank. The ensuing campaign event was viewed as something of a disaster. Riding around in a tank with a wide grin and gigantic helmet conveyed precisely the opposite image the Dukakis campaign had hoped to project. It was a goofy image, and his opponents seized on it to portray him as unready to be the commander and chief of the armed forces.[16]

★ PRESIDENTIAL ELECTIONS AS REFERENDUMS ★

Are presidential elections referendums on the party in power? Partially, but this is more true of some elections than others. When an incumbent president runs for reelection to a second term, he generally defends his record over the previous four years against attacks from his opponent. The president's opponent, meanwhile, seeks to make the case that the incumbent president had failed the country on the major issues of the day—and that he, the challenger, would be the stronger president.

However, elections are not simply "yes or no" referendums on the president or party in power. The voters certainly take a hard look at the challengers, and size them up. In other words, dissatisfaction with the governing party or president is usually not sufficient to turn the current president out of office. Generally, the challenger must meet a certain threshold of "acceptability"— the voters must be convinced that they can do the job.

In 2004, President George W. Bush had historically low approval ratings for a president about to be reelected.[17] In fact, he became the first president since Harry S. Truman to be re- elected with an approval rating below 50 percent. Keenly aware of their candidate's tenuous footing, the Bush campaign moved aggressively to define John Kerry in the eyes of the public early on in the campaign. They hammered Kerry relentlessly as an equivocator who shifted his positions with the political winds. U.S. involvement in the war in Iraq was a central issue in the 2004 campaign, and the Bush campaign attacked Kerry as unfit to lead a nation during wartime.

While responding to a question pertaining to an $87 billion war funding bill, Kerry committed a gaffe that would come back to haunt him throughout the campaign—and would be featured prominently in a Bush campaign ad. Kerry said: "I actually voted for the $87 billion before I voted against it." (Kerry was trying to explain that he voted in favor of the war-funding bill in committee, but voted against it when the bill reached the Senate floor for a final vote. Needless to say, the nuance of his explanation was lost in translation.)

While the electorate was clearly open to the possibility of replacing Bush as president in 2004, they did not see fit to replace him with Senator Kerry. Bush carried 51 percent of the national popular vote to Kerry's 48 percent, and won a close but clear-cut victory in the state of Florida. He also improved upon his previous electoral vote showing by winning New Mexico and Iowa—both of which had narrowly gone for Al Gore in 2000.

When a president is running for reelection, that campaign can be considered at least partly a referendum on the incumbent White House occupant. A sitting president running for a second term always defends and boasts about his accomplishments during the previous four years. This is much less true of elections in which there is no incumbent president seeking the office. In 2000, Vice President Al Gore declared during his acceptance speech at the Democratic National Convention: "We're electing a new president. And I stand here tonight as my own man, and I want you to know me for who I truly am."[18]

Gore's message was clear: His candidacy did not represent a bid for a third term for Bill Clinton. Some Democrats criticized this strategy, as Clinton was quite popular in the year leading up to the 2000 presidential election. Less surprising, however, was John McCain's effort in 2008 to distance himself from President George W. Bush. Bush had become deeply unpopular—and was sometimes described as an albatross around McCain's neck.

During a presidential debate, Obama tied McCain to Bush's

legacy, as he had done repeatedly throughout the campaign. McCain responded: "Senator Obama, I am not President Bush. If you want to run against President Bush, you should have run four years ago."[19] Despite this sharp rebuke, McCain was never able to overcome voter dissatisfaction with the Bush administration and the Republican Party—and he lost to Obama in the general election.

★ THE INCUMBENT: A PRESIDENT AND A CANDIDATE ★

When a sitting president runs for reelection, he or she must balance the demands of the White House with those of the campaign trail. It is a balancing act. If a president spends too much time campaigning, he or she can be accused of neglecting the duties of the Oval Office. Conversely, a president would surely be criticized as out-of-touch if he were to ignore demands that he get out of Washington and spend time with average voters.

THE ROSE GARDEN STRATEGY

One way presidents try to get reelected is to employ what is known as a "Rose Garden Strategy." The White House Rose Garden is located outside the Oval Office, and this strategy refers to a campaign run primarily from the White House in order to project leadership and stature. The idea is to appear *presidential,* and make one's opponent appear small by comparison.

A Rose Garden Strategy can prove risky and even unwise in a political environment in which the public seems ready for change, and favors an "outsider" as president. In fact, with Washington DC chronically unpopular with the electorate, presidential candidates frequently try to tar their opponents as "Washington insiders" while selling themselves as outsiders and agents of change.

★ EXTERNAL FACTORS IN PRESIDENTIAL CAMPAIGNS ★

Incumbent presidents and challengers can find themselves buoyed or hampered by factors partially or fully beyond their control. Economic conditions play a major role in presidential campaigns, and have allowed presidents to coast to reelection landslides—or forced them into early retirement. A low unemployment rate is nearly always a boon to the party in power, and an incumbent president will surely do all he can to take credit for it. Conversely, high unemployment puts the party and president in power on the defensive, and he must explain why efforts to jumpstart the nation's economy have failed.

In 1980, President Jimmy Carter lost his bid for reelection by a landslide margin to then-California Governor Ronald Reagan amid high unemployment and rampant inflation. Four years later, unemployment was still historically high—at just over 7 percent. But it had fallen sharply and rapidly from 10.8 percent,[20] and Reagan was able to convince the country that his vision had set the country on a path to prosperity. He was reelected in a historic, sweeping victory in which he carried forty-nine states.

More recently, the financial crisis of 2008 upended that year's presidential election. At first, the crisis didn't seem to favor one candidate over the other. But McCain's response to the situation—to suspend his campaign and threaten to withdraw from a scheduled debate—made him appear impulsive and unpredictable. By contrast, Obama appeared measured, calm, and steady.

Just as Obama seemed to benefit from the financial crisis of 2008, John Kerry supporters believe their candidate was hurt by a video released by Osama bin Laden the weekend before the 2004 election. The video guaranteed that terrorism was the central and defining issue in voters minds going into Election Day, and polls showed that the public trusted Bush over Kerry on that issue by a significant margin.

Appearing on Meet the Press, Kerry reflected on the role the tape played in his loss to Bush: "I believe that 9/11 was the central deciding issue in this race," he said. "And the tape—we were rising in the polls up until the last day when the tape appeared. We flat-lined the day the tape appeared and went down on Monday."[21]

★ THE PRESIDENTIAL DEBATES ★

In the autumn of a presidential election year, the major candidates traditionally meet face-to-face for a series of televised debates. Whether such debates have a decisive impact on the election results is itself open for debate, but they are generally broadcast by all of the major television networks. They are also closely analyzed by political reporters and pundits.

Presidential debates are generally hosted by a moderator, or a team of moderators who ask questions of the candidates. Depending on the rules of each particular debate—which are negotiated and agreed upon beforehand by the campaigns—the participants may make opening and closing statements.

Prior to the debates, the campaigns haggle over even the tiniest details with respect to the ground rules. Prior to the 2004 presidential debates, the Bush campaign demanded that the two candidates' lecterns be no more than fifty inches tall and spaced ten feet apart from one another. The reason? Bush's team was concerned that the height difference between the candidates (Kerry at six feet four, was five inches taller than Bush) would work to the Massachusetts Democrat's advantage. With the lecterns closer to the ground and farther apart, the height difference was less noticeable. The Bush campaign also rejected a demand from Kerry's team that the temperature of the room be set to 70 degrees Fahrenheit. Bush advisors had watched old tapes of debates from Kerry's U.S. Senate campaigns, and noticed that he had a tendency to sweat.[22]

In 1960, Massachusetts Senator and Democratic presidential nominee John F. Kennedy debated Vice President Richard Nixon, the Republican nominee. This was the first televised presidential debate, and it was the beginning of an important tradition in American presidential campaigns. While Kennedy and Nixon debated each other four times, the first debate was by far the most memorable and consequential. In 1960, television was still a relatively new medium, and politicians were unaccustomed to it. While Nixon certainly displayed mastery of the issues before the country, Kennedy—whom Republicans had criticized as too inexperienced—held his own. More importantly, television was unkind to Nixon's 5 o'clock shadow and sweaty forehead. Nixon had also been recovering from the flu, which made him appear both pale and gaunt. He had refused to wear any makeup, which could have improved his rather sickly appearance.

This was all in stark contrast to the youthful handsome senator from Massachusetts. Kennedy, who had been campaigning in California, appeared tanned and well rested. Those who had listened to the debate on the radio viewed Nixon as having given the stronger debate performance. But among those who watched on television, Kennedy was the clear winner.[23]

In general, only the Democratic and Republican presidential nominees are invited to participate in the debates. Perennial third party candidate Ralph Nader is excluded from the debates every four years, much to the chagrin of his supporters. In 1992, however, independent candidate Ross Perot—who was on the general election ballot in all fifty states and received 19 percent of the popular vote nationwide on Election Day—was permitted to participate. Perot was a billionaire Texas businessman who made the federal budget deficit the central issue in his campaign.

Perot was also difficult to label politically. He supported abortion rights and opposed gun control laws. He had adamantly opposed U.S. involvement in the 1991 Gulf War with Iraq, and was a proponent of expanding the federal government's war on illegal drugs. He embraced a tax on gasoline, and opposed trade agreements—arguing that they resulted in job losses domestically. Thus, his positions on issues appealed to both Democrats and Republicans who had become disenchanted with the two major political parties. And voter surveys found that his candidacy drew votes equally from then-Arkansas Governor Bill Clinton and President George H. W. Bush.

THE TOWN HALL DEBATE

In 1992, the major presidential candidates met for a debate unlike any American viewers had seen before. Questions would be posed not by a moderator or a team of journalists, but by citizens. While the questions were prescreened, members of the audience were allowed to ask a question of one of the presidential candidates, and all were invited to weigh in. This format was considered a boon to Bill Clinton, whose political skills were well suited to a more personal, less formal interaction with voters.

President Bush, however, did not fare nearly as well. Bush, as he would later admit, was not a fan of debates in general. In his view, they were staged events that offered little in the way of substance or meaningful policy discussions. As he would later tell PBS's Jim Lehrer, the debates were "showbiz."

During this town hall debate with Clinton and Perot, Bush was caught on camera looking at his wristwatch on two occasions. This seemingly minor display of boredom or impatience received considerable coverage in the news media. Moreover, the incident squared with one of the Democrats' major lines of attack against Bush—that he was out of touch and uninterested in the concerns of average voters.[24]

The town hall debate has since become something of an institution, and has been replicated in every subsequent presidential campaign.

Do Presidential Debates Affect Elections?

This question is difficult to answer definitively. Moreover, it would be even harder to quantify the effect of debates on the final vote on Election Day. Debates do seem to reinforce existing media narratives about a candidate—and therefore can put a spotlight on their strengths and weaknesses. In the case of President George H. W. Bush, the debates—particularly the town hall debate—reinforced an existing narrative that he was out of touch and did not empathize with Americans who were struggling.

In 2008, Republican presidential nominee John McCain

was arguably hampered by a similar dynamic. Barack Obama's campaign had repeatedly attacked McCain as "erratic." His actions surrounding the presidential debate only seemed to lend credence to Obama's criticism. Following a nationwide financial meltdown that upended national politics in the fall of 2008, McCain hastily assembled a press conference in which he announced he was suspending his campaign for president to deal with the crisis. He also announced that he would not participate in the first debate.

Obama—along with political commentators and many in the press—criticized McCain's behavior as inexplicable, and even bizarre. When Obama refused to back out of the first debate, McCain reversed course and decided to attend. During the first debate, McCain pointedly did not look at Obama once. This made him appear edgy and even hostile, and his performance was greeted by harsh criticism in the media. In addition, McCain seemed unaware of the split screen that repeatedly showed him grimacing while his opponent was speaking.[25]

In 2008, McCain's age—he was seventy-two, while Obama was forty-seven—also dogged him on the campaign trail. In fact, McCain's campaign team believed that Democratic attacks that he was "erratic" and "losing his bearings" were coded allusions to his age. (Obama's team countered that these characterizations spoke to McCain's temperament, not age.)[26] But it undoubtedly didn't help matters when McCain was seen wandering around the stage—sometimes in front of Obama while he was speaking—during the town hall debate. Late-night comedy shows, including *Saturday Night Live*, seized on the footage to mock the Republican hopeful.[27]

In 2000, Gore found himself under attack for his first debate performance against George W. Bush. Gore, who was often criticized for perceived pomposity, repeatedly sighed loudly into his microphone as Bush was speaking. Another Republican attack on Gore charged that he lacked authenticity, and continually "reinvented" himself. Gore's behavior seemed to corroborate this charge when, after being criticized for his aggressive performance in the first debate, he appeared noticeably subdued and conciliatory toward Bush in the second. Yet in the third and final meeting between the two candidates, Gore once again employed a highly assertive debating style.

At one point, Gore approached Bush as he was speaking. The move was visually awkward and gave the appearance of physical intimidation.*28 Mid-sentence, Bush acknowledged Gore's close physical proximity with a terse nod. The audience laughed, and Bush continued with his answer. Gore received much criticism for this performance in the media, and reinforced an existing media narrative that Bush was the more "likable" candidate.

★ PUBLIC OPINION POLLS ★

For better or for worse, public opinion polls play a prominent role in presidential elections. Generally speaking, there are two types of public opinion surveys: public polls and private polls. Private polls are commissioned by campaigns. Thus, a campaign can choose to release the poll if it has good news. If a private poll shows a candidate losing badly, his campaign will likely not release the poll to the general public.

Public polls, meanwhile, are not affiliated with any campaign. They may be commissioned by newspapers, radio sta-

---

* After the 2000 town hall style presidential debate, Bush's mother (who was also the former First Lady), Barbara Bush, remarked that Gore had "sort of scared" her. "I thought he was gonna hit George," she reportedly remarked.

tions, or outside political groups. One of the oldest independent pollsters is Gallup, a respected name whose surveys receive considerable attention in the press.

Campaigns tend to tout polls that show their candidate leading, and find fault with those showing them behind. Consumers of political news need to be somewhat on their guard; not all polls are created equal. A poll that may receive considerable attention from a campaign—or even a reputable news organization—may be flawed. In some cases, polls may use statistical methods that are neither valid nor reliable. Polls based on an unusually small sample size are often questionable. Polls that only release a "topline" number (such as "Smith Leads Parker 52 percent to 46 percent")—should be suspect. In other words, polls that do not release more detailed information on subsamples (such as how the two candidates are polling among voters over sixty-five, female voters, etc.) should be approached with caution. Such information on subsamples is referred to as a poll's "internals."

Why is all of this important? Bad polling misinforms the public.* Often, news organizations (even responsible ones) are not sufficiently discriminating when reporting on polls. Thus, it is important to know how to distinguish good polls from bad polls.

---

* Research 2000, a once widely used pollster, was accused in 2010 of fabricating its public opinion surveys. The liberal Web site Daily Kos, had hired this organization to conduct polling on the 2008 presidential race as well as 2010 congressional campaigns. After uncovering a number of suspicious anomalies in Research 2000's polling, a team of statisticians compiled a report for Daily Kos's founder contending that the polling firm's work could not possibly be legitimate. Their views were echoed by other well-known and respected pollsters. Daily Kos fired the polling firm, which soon became effectively defunct. Still, it had published hundreds of polls on races throughout the country that received press coverage from trusted sources.[29]

★ HOW DO VOTERS RESPOND TO PRESIDENTIAL ★ CAMPAIGNS?

While some voters pay more attention to presidential campaigns than others—and some people are more likely than others to go to the polls on Election Day—the segment of the electorate that is up for grabs in any general election is relatively small.

Only three times since 1940 has any Democratic or Republican candidate received less than 40 percent of the vote. On two of those occasions—1964 and 1972—the presidential contest featured one exceptionally weak candidate (Barry Goldwater in 1964 and George McGovern in 1972). This strongly suggests that at least 80 percent of the American electorate remains fairly stable in their voting preferences for president. (The third occasion was the 1992 presidential election, in which President George H. W. Bush received only 37.5 percent of the popular vote. That election, however, is not quite comparable to the others as it was a three-way race between Bush, Clinton, and Perot.)[30]

Presidential candidates have two objectives with respect to voters: make sure their committed supporters show up to the polls in large numbers, and win over as many undecided voters as possible. And the two political parties only see significant defections when their candidate is viewed as politically extreme (as was the case with both Goldwater and McGovern). If one candidate is widely viewed as unable to win, supporters of his political party may stay home on Election Day, seeing no reason to go to the polls. Needless to say, this is a nightmare for the party experiencing a depressed voter turnout.

Thus, many voters—namely those who are committed Democrats and committed Republicans—will not be swayed by what happens over the course of a presidential campaign. They are died-in-the-wool partisans.

One might think that the voters who pay the closest attention to presidential campaigns are the swing voters—after all, they make up the part of the electorate that is most likely to be swayed by campaigns. This is not necessarily the case. A committed, partisan Democratic or Republican voter might pay very close attention to the campaign, watching as many speeches as possible, and checking the latest polling data to see who is ahead in the key states. This type of voter watches the race for the White House so closely because he or she is invested in the outcome. In other words, highly partisan voters believe very strongly in their candidate, and want to see that person win.

Swing voters can also be very politically astute, and might follow campaigns very closely. They may have strongly held views but not identify with the Democratic or Republican parties. They may agree with the Democrats on certain issues, and with the Republicans on others. They may also simply be nonpolitical. They may not be interested in politics or government. On what basis then do such voters choose a president? Undoubtedly, questions relating to a candidate's character and personality can be quite important. Sometimes, voters have a visceral reaction to candidates, and it has little to do with their positions on issues. They may vote for a candidate based on a belief that they are of superior moral character when compared to his or her opponent. Or they may simply feel more comfortable with one particular candidate, and find him or her easier to relate to.

As mentioned earlier, these voters can also be swayed by external factors—particularly news events in the final stage of the campaign. In 2008, independent voters swung to Obama in the wake of the financial crisis that took center stage in the final weeks of the presidential race.[31]

★ HOW CAMPAIGNS HAVE CHANGED SINCE 1792 ★

Not surprisingly, campaigns have changed considerably since George Washington was elected as the nation's first president in 1789. First, voting was a privilege enjoyed by the elite, not the right of every American. Women and African Americans were barred from voting. In fact, voting was the exclusive right of white male property owners.

Women did not receive the right to vote until the Nineteenth Amendment to the Constitution was ratified in 1920. In 1870, the Fifteenth Amendment to the constitution prohibited voting restrictions based on race. However, blacks continued to be systematically disenfranchised until the enactment of the Voting Rights Act of 1965. Following the admission of new frontier states such as Ohio and Tennessee to the Union in the late 1700s and early 1800s, states began embracing a more participatory form of democracy, and allowed all male citizens to vote. This more populist brand of democracy was embodied in Andrew Jackson, a Tennessean who served two terms as president. While he was known as a political champion of the "common man," Jacksonian democracy did not extend to the rights of African Americans: He was a steadfast supporter of slavery.

The first presidential campaigns also differed from modern ones in that candidates did not travel around the country stumping for votes. Such activities were considered beneath the dignity of a statesman, and they left campaigning to surrogates.

In the first two presidential elections, Washington essentially ran unopposed. The only question was who would become vice president. (As the second place finisher in the Electoral College, John Adams was elected vice president, an office he would hold during both of Washington's terms as president.) The election of

1796 saw the first truly competitive presidential election, and the beginning of American political parties. With George Washington leaving office, Vice President John Adams ran under the Federalist ticket against Thomas Jefferson, who ran as a Democratic Republican.

While Adams and Jefferson did not campaign on their own behalves, their surrogates fought an acrimonious battle in the press, with each side engaging in truly vitriolic personal attacks against the other. Jefferson supporters, for example, attacked Adams as having a "hideous, hermaphroditical character." Adams loyalists called Jefferson a "mean-spirited, low-lived fellow, the son of a half-breed Indian squaw." While much has changed over the course of more than two centuries of presidential campaigns, negativity and nasty campaign attacks are clearly nothing new.[32]

SLOGANS

Slogans have become commonplace in politics and presidential campaigns. Historians trace this practice back to the candidacy of William Henry Harrison, who was elected president in 1840 after losing the 1836 election to Martin Van Buren. Harrison's campaign slogan played on his nickname ("Tippecanoe") and his running mate (John Tyler): "Tippecanoe and Tyler Too." Harrison's campaign also used a political attack by his opponent to his advantage, turning it into a slogan. Van Buren supporters contended that Harrison would have liked nothing more than to live out his days in a log cabin drinking hard cider. Harrison supporters responded by attacking Van Buren as a wealthy elitist, and touting their man as the "log cabin and hard cider candidate."[33] Harrison won the election, but died on his thirty-second day in office from complications of pneumonia.

★ THE RAILROAD, WHISTLE STOP TOURS, ★ AND POPULIST CAMPAIGNS

The completion of the Transcontinental Railroad in 1869 gave rise to a major change in presidential campaigning some twenty-five years later. In 1896, Democratic presidential candidate William Jennings Bryan introduced the "whistle stop tour" into presidential campaigns. Bryan—a man of extraordinary oratorical gifts—toured the country by rail, giving speeches to crowds from the rear of the train.[34] While he lost the election to William McKinley, his campaign had a lasting impact on presidential politics. Indeed, he paved the way for a more populist campaigning style that was embraced by future presidents—particularly Democrats in the New Deal era. (Harry Truman embarked on one of the most famous whistle stop tours on the way to an upset victory over Thomas Dewey in 1948.)

TELEVISION

As mentioned earlier, television played a major role in the 1960 presidential election between John F. Kennedy and Richard M. Nixon. While the 1952 and 1956 campaigns had seen the first candidate-sponsored television commercials, the Kennedy/Nixon contest was the first time the American public had the opportunity to see two candidates meet face-to-face on their TV screens. It also marked a turning point in that candidates were now exposed to the public through an entirely new medium. Candidates who were at ease in front of a camera enjoyed an advantage over those who were less comfortable in that setting. Ronald Reagan, who had been a highly successful actor prior to entering politics, clearly benefited from his comfort and familiarity with the cameras.

Until 1971, Americans were not constitutionally eligible to vote until they were twenty-one years of age. Not surprisingly, the many young people who became heavily involved in the 1968 presidential campaign—many of them loyal to Senator Eugene McCarthy—believed a voting age of twenty-one was grossly unfair. After all, they were eligible to be drafted into the military to fight during the Vietnam War, but were not eligible to vote. In 1971 the Twenty-sixth Amendment to the constitution guaranteed all Americans eighteen years of age or older the right to vote in elections.

The Internet also transformed political campaigns—as became evident in the 2004 and 2008 presidential races. The Web allowed candidates to reach voters in a new medium and raise vast, previously unthinkable sums of money. Howard Dean, an obscure governor of Vermont, rode a wave of Democratic discontent over the Iraq War to front-runner status in the Democratic primaries—before crashing and burning in truly spectacular fashion. However, he was a pioneer of Internet fundraising, and Barack Obama would revolutionize this model four years later. In fact, he raised more than half a billion dollars online from more than three million donors. This made up more than two thirds of his record total of $745 million in 2008.[35]

The Internet also enabled candidates to connect and communicate with voters through e-mail lists, political blogs, and later "new media" social networking venues such as Facebook and Twitter.

The Internet, however, also forces candidates to be on their guard constantly. If a candidate is recorded saying something impolitic, that ill-conceived remark will be viewed on YouTube by millions of people within hours. Why does this matter? It causes candidates to run highly cautious, controlled campaigns. While politicians are often criticized for a lack of authenticity and a lack of courage, an Internet-driven political culture reinforces this dynamic. In other words, presidential campaigns have become even more scripted, and less bold.

EXAMINING OUR ELECTORAL PROCESS

As each presidential campaign draws to a close, reporters, historians, and political pundits begin to examine what has unfolded over the last two years. Understandably, many wonder aloud whether the public was well served by the manner in which we, as a nation, choose a president. Inevitably, they ask why "voter turnout" was so low. "Voter turnout," of course, refers to the number of Americans eligible to vote who actually show up to cast a ballot. Prior to 2004, turnout had been steadily declining since 1968, when nearly 62 percent of these eligible voters voted. In 1996, voter turnout fell to 49 percent, its lowest level since 1924. Voter turnout spiked in 2004 and 2008, however, to 60 percent and 62 percent respectively.*

---

* Voter turnout estimates vary considerably depending on the metric used to determine the total population eligible to participate in elections. Some use a "Voting Age Population" model, which measures the percentage of the total number of people who were old enough to vote who showed up to the polls. This metric is problematic, because it includes felons and noncitizens in its total—and these populations cannot vote. The "Voter-Eligible Population" (VEP) metric, first used by Michael P. McDonald and Samuel L. Popkin, is far more accurate. This measures the total voting-age population minus noncitizens and felons. The figures cited in the paragraph above refer to VEP. One may also encounter an estimate of voter turnout that simply measures the percentage of registered voters who cast ballots on Election Day. This metric disregards the millions of Americans who are eligible to vote but are not registered. It dramatically overstates voter turnout (because

Presidential campaigns and political parties frequently try to register new voters in the hope that new registrations will improve their performance on Election Day. (Independent civic-minded groups also try to register new voters, striving for a more engaged electorate and participatory democracy.) However, increased voter registration does not necessarily translate into higher voter turnout. Despite more than 10 million new voter registrations in 2008, voter turnout increased only slightly from 2004.[37] Why the discrepancy? It is much easier to register to vote than to wait on long lines at the polls on Election Day.[38]

The Electoral College is another perennial target of criticism. Since the Electoral College narrows the battlefield to approximately fifteen states, voters in Florida and Ohio receive more attention and are more influential than those in New York or Utah. In addition, critics of the Electoral College correctly point out that it has a tendency to greatly exaggerate a candidate's margin of victory. Despite Barack Obama's 53 percent to 46 percent margin over John McCain in the national popular vote, the Electoral College results produced a lopsided Obama victory of 365–173 (a more than two-to-one margin). Perhaps most importantly, the Electoral College leaves open the possibility of electing a president who was rejected by a plurality of the American people (as happened in 2000). Continuing to use such a system for electing a president in the modern era, critics argue, is undemocratic.

The question of how campaigns should be financed continually vexes those concerned about the integrity of our electoral process. In the United States, campaigns are funded largely

---

those not registered to vote are not included in the total), and thus is not terribly useful.[36]

through private donations. Many critics of this system favor total public financing of elections, in which each candidate receives the same sum of taxpayer money. Candidates would be prohibited from spending more than what they were allocated. (Candidates who abide by campaign spending limits do receive public financing. Candidates can, however, opt out of the public financing system and raise unlimited sums of money. In addition, outside groups can spend heavily on a candidate's behalf.) Supporters of this system argue that it would allow candidates to succeed or fail on the strength or weakness of their message rather than their fundraising abilities.

Critics of publicly funded elections contend that taxpayer money should not be spent on politicians or their campaigns. In fact, some critics go so far as to deride the very idea of public financing as a welfare program for politicians. Such critics also regard limitations on Americans' ability to donate to candidates as an attack on their freedom of expression.

While Congress has passed a number of campaign finance laws to regulate fundraising activities, these laws have so far failed to effectively guard against scandal or reduce the influence of money in politics. In the mid 1970s, Congress passed legislation limiting federal campaign contributions to candidates. Yet so-called "soft money"—contributions made to political parties rather than directly to candidates—remained unlimited. In 2002, Senators John McCain (R-AZ) and Russ Feingold (D-WI) pushed legislation through Congress banning soft money contributions. With misgivings, President George W. Bush signed the measure into law. Despite the 2002 law, contributions to independent groups (527's, which were explained earlier) remained unlimited. These groups remain free to spend heavily in campaigns.

So-called "bundlers" have also emerged as a cause for concern with respect to campaign fundraising. Bundlers are well-connected individuals who compile campaign contributions from friends, family members, and business associates on behalf of one candidate. As the costs of running a national campaign have soared, candidates have increasingly turned to bundlers to raise the necessary funds required to remain competitive. Critics argue that bundling lacks the transparency necessary to guarantee clean elections; candidates are not required to disclose information about their bundlers.

One such bundler, Norman Hsu, proved to be a major embarrassment to Hillary Clinton's 2008 presidential campaign. Hsu, who had been bundling contributions for Clinton, was a federal fugitive who was charged with violating campaign finance laws by making contributions under other people's names. He was also accused of pressuring investors to donate to his preferred candidates and defrauding his investors in a $20 million Ponzi scheme.[39] Clinton returned more than $800,000 associated with Hsu's fundraising activities.

Every four years, the question of a viable third party candidacy arises. In order to receive public financing (matching funds from the federal government), third parties must have received at least 5 percent of the popular vote in the previous election. Third party candidates, however, rarely meet this threshold. In the run-up to the presidential debates, third party candidates always demand to be included, although they are rarely permitted to participate. (Ross Perot in 1992 was the exception. However, he was clearly a major force in that election. At one point, he led in the polls, with Bush polling in second place and Clinton third.[40])

While Americans regularly claim fatigue and even disgust

with the two major political parties, they rarely seem to take third party candidates seriously. Perot's 19 percent of the popular vote in 1992 was the most viable third party presidential candidacy in recent history.

In the 2012 presidential election, a new type of 527 has received considerable attention in the news media and from government watchdog groups. These organizations are known as "super political action committees," or "super PACs," although they are technically called "independent expenditure-only committees." These super PACs became legal following two key court decisions. In Citizens *United v. Federal Election Commission,* a Supreme Court ruling barred the federal government from limiting "independent" political spending by corporations and unions. In the second decision, the DC Circuit Court of Appeals ruled that the federal government could not limit financial contributions to such independent groups.

These two decisions effectively upended campaign finance law, and gave rise to what are now referred to as super PACs. While super PACs must technically remain independent from candidates' campaigns, the prohibition on coordination has become something of a joke. For example, former Massachusetts Governor Mitt Romney, who is seeking the Republican nomination for president in 2012, has claimed that his campaign is not coordinating with Restore Our Future, an independent super PAC running ads attacking his opponents. Yet the person running that super PAC is Carl Forti—who served as Romney's political director during his 2008 presidential campaign. Comedian Stephen Colbert sought to draw attention to this issue by starting his own super PAC, "Americans for a Better Tomorrow, Tomorrow."

He then declared his candidacy for president and turned his super PAC over to his longtime friend and host of *The Daily Show,* Jon Stewart. The Colbert super PAC was then renamed: "The Definitely Not Coordinating With Stephen Colbert Super PAC."

CHAPTER
☆ 5 ☆

ELECTION DAY

After what may feel like an eternity, the long grueling journey of our modern presidential campaign finally comes to an end on the first Tuesday after the first Monday in November. The candidates show up at the local polling place where they are registered to vote and smile for the cameras before entering the voting booth. This is often their last public appearance until a winner has been declared.

The campaigns monitor voter turnout as such information becomes available. In Ohio, a battleground state in every competitive presidential election, Democrats will closely watch turnout in their strongholds of Cleveland, Columbus, and Cincinnati. Republicans will monitor turnout in the rural areas and suburbs that form their political base in the state.

In Florida, Democrats hope their supporters in South Florida counties show up in droves. Republicans, meanwhile, watch the Panhandle. In addition, both camps look at the most competitive, and often suburban counties (such as Bucks County in Pennsylvania) to determine which candidate is performing more strongly among swing constituencies. The campaigns also closely study "bellwether" counties—counties in which the vote for president mirrors that statewide vote (or in a few cases, the national vote) in election after election.

Given the importance of strong turnout in key counties,

even the weather can be a cause for concern among campaign staffers monitoring the numbers. For example, if bad weather causes a few thousand voters in Philadelphia or Kansas City to stay home, it could conceivably influence the outcome of a close statewide vote.

At the local level, party operatives and volunteers are busy arranging for their supporters to get to the polls, and working as "pollwatchers." Pollwatchers represent a political party and candidate, and monitor the voting process on Election Day to ensure that eligible citizens are permitted to vote—and that those who are not eligible to vote are not permitted to do so. To be clear, the *act of voting* is private—no one monitors voters while they cast their ballots in the voting booth.

Other volunteers—some working for specific candidates and others for state parties—make phone calls to voters in an effort to maximize turnout among their supporters. Sometimes, a voter might receive three or four phone calls on Election Day. (This can be rather irritating for many people, but one hopes it does not serve as a deterrent to voting.)

★ THE VOTERS ★

For some voters, Election Day may be extraordinarily exciting. For political junkies, it is a momentous event. For others, it may simply mark the end of a seemingly never-ending stream of negative ads, hokey political slogans, and disingenuous posturing. For this type of voter, the choice is between the lesser of two evils. Regardless, the voting public piles into their local polling stations, which are often schools or churches.

Lines can be long, depending on the level of interest in the election. Lower income communities may experience longer waits to vote because their local government cannot afford a sufficient number of voting machines to accommodate local residents. Such disparities among different communities may affect turnout, and remain unresolved issues of concern.

In addition, some states close their polling places much earlier than others. In Vermont and Kentucky, the polls close at 7 p.m. EST (except in Eastern Kentucky, where the polls close at 6 p.m.). In New York State, they close at 9 p.m. EST. Later poll closings can make it easier for people with inflexible work hours to vote. Sometimes, a judge will issue a court order to keep polling stations open later if long lines materialize around the time such stations are scheduled to close.

ABSENTEE VOTING

Some voters are unable to make it to the polls on Election Day but still wish to cast a ballot. They may be unavoidably out of town on Election Day, or may be physically unable (due to illness or injury) to make it to their polling place. These individuals may use "absentee ballots," which are filled out at home and returned by mail. Some states require absentee voters to have a valid reason for failing to vote in person at the polls. Others have virtually no restrictions on absentee voting, and allow all registered voters to do so.

Oregon holds elections entirely by mail. Voters simply fill out their ballots and mail them in, and do not need to show up at all to polling places. Ballots are held until Election Day, and then opened and counted.

Residents of many states now have the option of voting early—weeks before Election Day. Proponents of early voting argue that it gives the public a greater opportunity to go to the polls, and therefore holds the promise of a more vibrant participatory democracy. Critics point out, however, that those who vote early may risk making an uninformed decision at the polls. For example, suppose that someone casts his or her vote on September 30. In the intervening period between late September and Election Day, any number of events could transpire. For example, the press could uncover a major scandal involving a candidate. Early voters could have cast their ballots for that candidate without having known about such a scandal. In a more extreme scenario, a major candidate could die before Election Day. If such a tragedy were to take place, early voters could have cast ballots for a candidate who was deceased.

Watching the Returns

As the polls begin to close around the country, Americans settle in to watch the returns. A large map of the United States looms over news anchors reporting new developments (or, just as likely, chatting to kill time in the absence of news). The early returns, which begin to trickle in around 7 p.m. are rarely illustrative of any major trends. Kentucky and Vermont are usually among the first to be called (Vermont for the Democrat and Kentucky for the Republican).

Throughout the night, the networks and cable news channels check in with campaign spokespeople, who invariably express confidence and cautious optimism. Even if a campaign spokesperson expects to be on the losing side of Election Night, he or she will try to remain upbeat in front of the camera. If their supporters believed that all hope was lost, they might decide that a trip to the polls was a fool's errand. Thus, campaign staffers put on a brave face for the public, even if things don't seem to be going their way.

In addition, news anchors will check in with reporters and electoral experts to shed light on any significant developments. In the crucial battleground of Ohio, how is the Democratic candidate faring in key, swing counties? What does voter turn-out look like in the cities when compared to turnout four years ago? In Florida, how is the Republican candidate performing in the northern part of the state compared with four years ago, when the Republican hopeful eked out a razor-thin victory in the Sunshine State?

If the networks project a winner in a state the moment the polls have closed, the winner's margin of victory was big enough to allow for a projection based on the exit polling alone. After the 2000 election, the networks have been far more careful when making a projection based on exit polling. Thus, if they call Pennsylvania for the Republican as soon as the polls closed at 8 p.m., this almost certainly means that the Republican carried Pennsylvania in a romp. Furthermore, a big victory in Pennsylvania—an important battleground state—likely portends a strong performance in other key states as well.

The 8 p.m. and 9 p.m. poll closings set loose an avalanche of electoral votes and, in all but the closest elections, begin to reveal the likely victor. Eight o'clock marks the closing of three key battleground states with sizable electoral vote totals: Florida (a fiercely contested battleground with 25 electoral votes), Pennsylvania (another key swing state), and Missouri, another bellwether state. Illinois also begins to report its returns at 8 p.m., but the Land of Lincoln generally falls in the Democratic column (barring a 1980-style GOP landslide).

At 9 p.m., returns begin to trickle in from the major electoral prizes of Michigan (a battleground state with 16 electoral votes), New York (a Democratic state with 29 electoral votes), Texas (a Republican-leaning state with 38 electors), as well as Wisconsin (10), Minnesota (10), and Colorado (9)—all key competitive states.

The night's biggest prize—California—does not begin to report its returns until 11 p.m. EST. While California is not a swing state—it has a distinct Democratic lean—it can seal the deal for a Democratic White House victory. In 2008, Barack Obama's victory was announced as soon as California's polls closed, although it had been clear he was headed for a national victory when he won Ohio much earlier in the evening.

★ THE CANDIDATES ★

Amid all the drama and commotion, the candidates can finally breathe—perhaps for the first time in well over a year. The campaign is over, and there are no more hands to shake, no more interviews, no more donors to call—at least for now. For the moment, they can retire from the spotlight and watch the returns with their closest aides and family members. Generally, the public does not see either of the candidates until it is time for the victory and concession speeches.

As the candidates huddle with their families and senior staff, they continually receive updates throughout the afternoon and evening. They are kept aware of exit polling throughout Election Day, as well as turnout in key areas. Of course, until the votes are actually counted, drawing conclusions from these results can lead candidates into a false sense of security—or even despair. On Election Day in 2004, Democratic strategist Bob Shrum looked over exit polling and concluded that his candidate, Massachusetts Senator John Kerry, had won. He had good reason to be optimistic. National exit polling showed Kerry defeating Bush by a 51–48 percent margin.[1] The actual result showed the reverse: Bush defeated Kerry, 51–48 percent.

A subsequent analysis showed that the exit polls had over-stated Kerry's support in twenty-six states. In fact, the exit polling showed Kerry winning most of the battleground states, including Florida and Ohio. After reviewing the exit polls, Shrum approached Kerry and (prematurely) addressed him as "Mr. President."[2] Just as in 2000, the exit polls were wrong. Bush carried Ohio, Florida, and was reelected to a second term.

ONE CANDIDATE TRIUMPHS, THE OTHER CONCEDES

Once one candidate claims 270 electoral votes, he or she can declare victory. Generally, the first order of business after an election has been called is the concession phone call: The loser phones the victor to concede the election and offer congratulations. The candidate who fell short then gives a concession speech, in which he or she thanks supporters and urges them to rally behind the nation's new president. Finally, the president-elect gives a victory speech to a crowd of supporters. He thanks the public, his supporters and volunteers, and tries to graciously offer words of appreciation for his vanquished rival.

The timing of a concession speech can be a difficult matter. In landslide elections, the networks may project a winner very early in the night. Thus, a candidate may be declared the winner before the polls close on the West Coast. In 1980, the network called the election for Ronald Reagan very early— NBC called it at 8:15 p.m. More than an hour before the polls had closed in Western states, President Jimmy Carter publicly conceded defeat. Congressional Democrats—particularly those from California, Oregon, and Washington—were appalled and infuriated. With no reason to vote, depressed Democratic turnout in the West threatened to hurt the party up and down the ballot. Congressional Democrats—who were never fans of Carter to begin with—were enraged. House Speaker Tip O'Neil placed an angry call to Carter's congressional liaison.[3] While Carter may have wanted the night to be over, O'Neil had Democratic House seats in the West to worry about.

★ THE ELECTORAL MANDATE ★

A presidential candidate's first objective on Election Day is to win 270 electoral votes, thereby winning the presidency. Beyond an Electoral College victory, however, candidates hope to win an electoral mandate—a clear majority in both the Electoral College and the popular vote. Quite simply, a clear-cut victory is widely interpreted as a sign that the winner has been given a clear mandate to implement his or her agenda. A mandate is generally perceived by members of Congress and the media as a clear sign that the president-elect has won the confidence of the American people.

How significant must an electoral victory be to signal a popular mandate? This is a matter of opinion, as a mandate is in the eye of the beholder. If a candidate wins the presidency by a 51-49 percent margin, his party will argue that the president clearly has a mandate to govern and implement the policy agenda on which he ran. The opposition will argue that such a close election was a mandate for unity and compromise, and that the president-elect should trim his sails.

Following the 2000 election, Democrats argued that President George W. Bush lacked a mandate since he failed to win a majority of the popular vote. Their efforts to paint Bush as illegitimate were largely unsuccessful; the president succeeded in pushing massive tax cuts and sweeping education reform through Congress early in his first term. Republicans had argued that Bill Clinton lacked a popular mandate since he twice failed to win a majority of the popular vote in 1992 and 1996. (In both of those races, Ross Perot's presence in the race prevented Clinton from claiming a majority.)

The depth and breadth of a candidate's victory can also bolster their claims of a popular mandate. In 2008, Barack Obama won the popular vote by a 53–46 percent margin—a strong, clear victory to be sure—but not a landslide. Still, he won states that had not voted for a Democratic presidential candidate in half a century, including Virginia and Indiana. He also won huge victories in previously competitive states (61 percent of the vote in California and 58 percent in Washington State.) These factors contributed to the perception that Obama had won a mandate for change.

Of course, Ronald Reagan's sweeping victories in 1980 and 1984 were also interpreted as mandates for his conservative political agenda. This was reflected in his success in pushing his agenda through Congress, particularly in his first term. Despite Democratic control of the House of Representatives, Congress passed Reagan's sweeping tax cuts as well as his proposed increases in military spending.

President Lyndon B. Johnson was perhaps the clearest example of a president using a popular mandate to enact sweeping change. Following his landslide victory in 1964 over Barry Goldwater (61–39 percent in the popular vote, and a 486–52 Electoral College majority), Johnson signed historic civil rights legislation as well as bills that created Medicare (which guarantees medical care to the elderly) and Medicaid (which provides health insurance to the nation's poor).

★ A NEW PRESIDENT TAKES OFFICE ★

While Election Day takes place on the first Tuesday after the first Monday in November, the president-elect does not become president until he or she takes the oath of office on January 20. In between, an outgoing administration passes the reigns of power to the new one. This is known simply as the "presidential transition." In fact, when a sitting president calls the new president-elect on Election Night to offer his congratulations, it is customary for the soon-to-be ex-president to promise a "smooth transition."

A smooth transfer of power from one president to the next is crucial to ensuring that the business of the federal government continues to operate uninterrupted. During the presidential transition, the new president begins nominating members of his cabinet (such as the Secretary of State, Secretary of Defense, etc.) and names people to lead various government agencies. In short, he begins putting his team in place. In addition, members of the departing regime brief members of the new administration on important matters.

The transition is also an important period symbolically. Once a new president is elected, the sitting president is no longer viewed by the world as a national leader, although he is still the head of state for more than two and a half months. The outgoing president is now referred to as a "lame duck," a term that aptly describes his weakened stature. Conversely, the president-elect is widely viewed as the new leader of the United States—though he enjoys none of the legal authority of the presidency until Inauguration Day.

Following the 2008 presidential election, the transition between the administrations of George W. Bush and Barack Obama was noteworthy for its seamless and congenial nature.[4] Some presidential transitions, however, have not been so smooth. Following Herbert Hoover's loss to Franklin Delano Roosevelt, FDR refused to participate in a joint effort (sought by Hoover) to address the nation's downward economic spiral. Despite Hoover's entreaties, FDR believed a commitment to an economic program proposed during the transition period could tie his hands as president. This angered Hoover, and the two men had one of the most tempestuous relationships of any two outgoing and incoming presidents in history.[5]

Following the 2000 presidential election, Clinton administration employees vandalized the White House during the transition leading up to George W. Bush taking the oath of office. Unlike in 1932, these incidents were merely juvenile in nature, and had no consequences with respect to public policy. The damage, which totaled roughly $13,000, included missing "W" keys from computer keyboards (a reference to the incoming president's middle initial), as well as signs and voice-mail messages disparaging Bush.[6]

The presidential transition does not align perfectly with the swearing in of a new Congress. While the president assumes his office on January 20, members of the House and Senate are sworn in earlier in the month. Thus, there is often a nearly three-week period during which a new Congress serves along side a lame-duck president. This worked to President Obama's advantage following his election in 2008: With large majorities in the House and Senate, the Democratic-controlled Congress began passing legislation for Obama to sign even before he was sworn into office. (Six days before Obama was sworn into office, the House passed a major expansion of children's health insurance coverage that had been vetoed twice by President Bush but was supported by then-Senator Obama.)[7]

CHAPTER
☆ 6 ☆

Inauguration Day

On January 20, a huge crowd gathers in front of the United States Capitol as a new president is sworn into office. At 12:01 p.m., the outgoing president becomes a private citizen, and the president-elect becomes the leader of the free world. Inauguration Day is marked by parades, parties, balls and galas, and many other festivities.

While the day is undoubtedly more euphoric for the incoming president's political party, inaugurations are a nonpartisan affair. Members of both parties in Congress attend, as does the outgoing president and vice president. While January 20 can be a day of bitter cold in Washington DC, the swearing-in ceremony is held outdoors, in front of the Capitol building. The Chief Justice of the Supreme Court administers the oath of office as required by Article Two, Section One, Clause Eight of the U.S. Constitution.

The oath, which has been sworn by every president since George Washington, reads: "I do solemnly swear (or affirm) that I will faithfully execute the Office of President of the United States, and will to the best of my ability, preserve, protect and defend the Constitution of the United States."

While the words "So help me God" do not appear in the oath, every president has recited them since Washington.

While the administering of the oath of office is normally a routine affair, Chief Justice John Roberts flubbed the oath during

Barack Obama's inauguration in 2009, misplacing the word "faithfully." Obama's political opponents even charged that he was not legally sworn-in as president, although constitutional scholars confirmed that he had legally become president at 12:01 regardless of what had transpired during the administering of the oath. (Roberts administered the oath a second time the following day.)[1]

Following the oath of office, the president gives his inaugural address. This speech is a broad, thematic address in which the new president seeks to define his presidency and agenda in very general terms. Inaugural addresses are not policy speeches, and generally contain little in the way of specifics or legislative proposals. Rather, they focus on the major, overarching issues facing the country, and serve as an introduction between a nation and its new president. In a new president's inaugural address, the public is introduced to the president not as a candidate, but as their elected leader, their new head of state.

★ PAST INAUGURAL ADDRESSES ★

While many presidents have given forgettable inaugural addresses, there are a number of standouts. In 1961, President John F. Kennedy's inaugural address emphasized generational change and a commitment to human rights around the world:

> We dare not forget today that we are the heirs of that first revolution. Let the word go forth from this time and this place, to friend and foe alike, that the torch has been passed to a new generation of Americans—born in this century, tempered by war, disciplined by a hard and bitter peace, proud of our ancient heritage—and unwilling to

witness or permit the slow undoing of those human rights to which this nation has always been committed, and to which we are committed today at home and around the world.

Kennedy's address also appealed to sacrifice, volunteerism, and a notion of active, civic citizenship:

And so, my fellow Americans: ask not what your country can do for you—ask what you can do for your country. My fellow citizens of the world: ask not what America will do for you, but what together we can do for the freedom of man.[2]

While inaugural addresses can be lengthy and sweeping, they are also shaped by the environment in which they are delivered. FDR's fourth inaugural address—delivered in 1945 during the height of the Second World War—was given without the normal pomp and circumstance. At 558 words, it was extraordinarily brief. Roosevelt said:

We have learned that we cannot live alone, at peace; that our own well-being is dependent on the well-being of other nations far away. We have learned that we must live as men, not as ostriches, nor as dogs in the manger.

We have learned to be citizens of the world, members of the human community. . . .

The Almighty God has blessed our land in many ways. He has given our people stout hearts and strong arms with which to strike mighty blows for freedom and truth. He has given to our country a faith which has become the hope of all peoples in an anguished world.

So we pray to Him now for the vision to see our way clearly—to see the way that leads to a better life for ourselves and for all our fellow men—to the achievement of His will to peace on earth.[3]

In 1980, Ronald Reagan used his first inaugural address to argue for a more limited role for the federal government:

The economic ills we suffer have come upon us over several decades. They will not go away in days, weeks, or months, but they will go away. They will go away because we as Americans have the capacity now, as we've had in the past, to do whatever needs to be done to preserve this last and greatest bastion of freedom.

In this present crisis, government is not the solution to our problem; government is the problem. From time to time we've been tempted to believe that society has become too complex to be managed by self-rule, that government by an elite group is superior to government for, by, and of the people.[4]

In 1905, President Theodore Roosevelt told the nation: "We know that self-government is difficult. We know that no people needs such high traits of character as that people which seeks to govern its affairs aright through the freely expressed will of the freemen who compose it. But we have faith that we shall not prove false to the memories of the men of the mighty past. They did their work, they left us the splendid heritage we now enjoy. We in our turn have an assured confidence that we shall be able to leave this heritage unwasted and enlarged to our children and our children's children."[5]

As one can see from the excerpts above, inaugural addresses

are not wonky speeches that address the specifics of tax policy. Rather, new presidents take into account the mood of the country and strive to set the tone for the next four years.

Following the inaugural address, the outgoing president leaves the White House to begin life as a private citizen. The new president and First Lady (the president's spouse) make the much-anticipated journey down Pennsylvania Avenue from the Capitol Building to the White House—his home for the duration of his presidency. This inaugural parade has been an enduring tradition since Jefferson's second inaugural, although it has changed somewhat over time. Due to security concerns, presidents no longer walk the entire way, but rather ride in a heavily guarded limousine and get out to walk from time to time.

With the inauguration over, the business of governing begins. Over the next four years, the new president will be tested. He will be pressured by his staunch supporters to keep campaign promises and urged by opponents to compromise and even capitulate. He (or she) will face international crises that may prove to be entirely beyond his control. And in the clash between convictions and the constraints of reality, the new president seeks to earn his place in history.

☆ GLOSSARY ☆

ballot. A piece of paper or device on which a voter records his or her choice in an election. In presidential elections, we use ballots to record our votes for president, the House of Representatives, U.S. Senate, and other offices. In other elections, ballots may simply be used to cast votes for the local school board. A ballot can be as simple as slip of paper on which a voter marks the name of his or her preferred candidate(s), or as high-tech as touch-screen machine.

cabinet. The key group of advisors and policymakers that assist the president. This group of people, includes the vice president, the secretary of defense (who oversees military policy), the secretary of education (who is responsible for implementing, coordinating, and advocating on behalf of the administration's education policies and federal education law), and the attorney general (who is the nation's chief law enforcement officer and lawyer for the federal government). With the exception of the vice president (who is elected alongside the president), cabinet members are nominated by the president and must be confirmed by the U.S. Senate.

candidate. A person seeking a public office. One can be a candidate for president, Congress, the U.S. Senate, governor, mayor, or even local sheriff. Contrary to popular belief, dogcatcher is not an elective office.

caucus. With respect to U.S. presidential elections, caucuses refer to elections in which voters gather at local schools and churches to elect delegates loyal to their preferred candidates. In marked contract to secret ballot elections, caucuses are very public civic exercises, in which supporters advocate for their preferred candidates and try to win over undecided caucusgoers.

Congress. The legislative branch of the United States Government. Congress is made up of two legislative bodies—the House of Representatives and the Senate.

congressman. A member of the U.S. House of Representatives. See **Representative**.

dark horse. A political candidate who is usually unknown to the electorate and appears to have little chance of winning. Occasionally, dark horse candidates do far better than expected, and in some cases even win elections. The term's origin relates to an old English horse-racing trick, in which a jockey would disguise a fast horse by dying the color of its coat to disguise its identity. When this horse won, everyone was shocked.

general election. The stage of a presidential election in which the nominees of political parties face off against one another. Independent candidates also compete in the general election. The general election officially begins in the late summer—following the nominating conventions—and lasts until Election Day.

governor. The elected chief executive of a state. Much like a president, governors sign legislation (passed by state legislatures) into law—and veto bills that they oppose.

grassroots. The level of a political campaign that is closest to actual voters. A grassroots campaign is fueled by the enthusiasm of volunteers and supporters of a political candidate or party. Nearly all viable campaigns have an element of grassroots strategy—but some campaigns have grassroots support that is far stronger than others.

inauguration. The ceremony in which a new president is sworn into office following a presidential election. Inauguration Day in the United States in January 20th of any year following a presidential election. For example, following the 2012 presidential election, Inauguration Day will be held on January 20, 2013.

independent voter. A voter who is not registered or affiliated with a political party.

legislature. The branch of government that writes laws. The federal government's legislature is Congress, made up of the House and Senate. States also have their own legislatures, which write state laws. State legislatures often have a state senate and state house or assembly. City councils are another example of legislatures.

nominee. A political party's chosen candidate for elective office. The nominee is the official standard-bearer of a political party in an election.

nominating convention. A multiday event generally held in late summer of presidential election years in which political parties officially choose their candidates for president. After officially becoming a party's nominee, the candidate gives a speech before the full convention and formally "accepts" his or her party's nomination. The conventions mark the end of the primary season, and the official start of the general election campaign.

party member. Someone who is registered with a political party. When citizens register to vote, they have the option of becoming a member of a political party. Independent voters chose not to register with a party.

plank. A section of political party's platform. Each plank is devoted to a specific issue or policy.

platform. A political party's statement of values and policy on the issues facing the country. Sometimes referred to as a "manifesto."

plurality. The number of votes by which the first place finisher leads his or her closest rival in an election. For example, if Candidate A receives 45 percent of the vote, while B receives 41 percent, and C 14 percent, A will have won a plurality of votes cast—but not a majority (which require 50 percent plus one).

political party. A group of people organized around shared political beliefs and principles that tries to elect like-minded people to public office.

politician. A person who works in politics professionally. The term "politician" usually refers to individuals holding or seeking elective office, although it can also be used to describe people who work for political parties, candidates, or causes.

politics. Generally speaking, the processes and activities relating to governing. In the United States and many other countries, politics most often refers to the effort by political parties and candidates to win elections in order to obtain control of a government—thereby allowing those parties and candidates to enact public policies.

poll. A public opinion survey intended to determine the views of the public toward politicians and public policies. In elections, polls are conducted to gauge how much support each candidate has among the electorate.

polls. The place at which voters cast their ballots in elections. Schools, for example, are often used as polling places.

precinct. Essentially the smallest possible voting district in elections. The number of voters per precinct varies considerably.

president-elect. The candidate who won the presidential election but who has not yet been sworn into office as president. In the intervening period between Election Day and Inauguration Day, the victor is known as the "president-elect."

presidential primary election. State-level elections held to determine the nominees of political parties. Along with the caucuses, primary elections award delegates to candidates in each state's contest. The candidate with the most delegates at the end of the primary season becomes the party's nominee for president.

Note: Primary elections are also held for candidates for other offices (such as House and Senate).

representative. A member of the U.S. House of Representatives. The House has 435 members with full voting rights. (U.S. territories and the District of Columbia elect delegates to the House and the do not enjoy full voting privileges.) Each member represents a different district within a state. States with very small populations (such as Vermont) are represented by just one member in the House. The House is sometimes referred to as the "lower house" of Congress, or the "lower body."

senator. A member of the U.S. Senate. The Senate is comprised of one hundred members, and each state is represented by two senators—regardless of the state's population. All senators represent entire states (unlike House members, who represent districts within states). The Senate is sometimes referred to as the "upper house" of Congress, or the "upper body."

stump speech. A candidate's standard speech on the campaign trail, which changes little from day to day. This speech incorporates the candidate's core message.

third party. A political party other than the Democratic or Republican Parties. While third parties and their candidates can have an impact on elections, they rarely have a plausible chance of winning.

transition. The intervening period between Election Day and Inauguration Day. During this time, the current president prepares to pass the reigns of power to the president-elect and a new administration.

Each incoming president takes the following oath on Inauguration Day:

> I do solemnly swear (or affirm) that I will faithfully execute the office of President of the United States, and will to the best of my ability, preserve, protect and defend the Constitution of the United States.

While "So help me, God" is not technically part of the oath of office, it has become customary for new presidents to complete the oath with this phrase.

☆ PAST PRESIDENTIAL ELECTIONS ☆

YEAR	WINNING CANDIDATE (PARTY), EVs*	LOSING CANDIDATE (PARTY), EVs[1]
1789	George Washington (No party) 69	John Adams (No party), 34
1792	George Washington (No party) 132	John Adams (No party), 77
1796	John Adams (Federalist), 71	Thomas Jefferson (Democratic-Republican), 68
1800	Thomas Jefferson (Democratic-Republican), 73	Aaron Burr (Democratic-Republican), 73

---

* EV = Electoral Votes

1. While John Adams was technically the runner-up in America's first presidential election, he cannot accurately be called "the losing candidate." Rather, Washington was the Electoral College's unanimous choice for president. In the first four presidential elections, however, electors cast two votes on one ballot—one for president and one for vice president. Yet electors did not specify which candidate was their choice for president, and which was their choice for vice president. Thus, the candidate with the most electoral votes became president, while the second place finisher became VP. In this case, all 69 electors cast their vote for Washington to be president. For vice president, Adams received the most votes (34). As a result, he was elected vice president.

1804	Thomas Jefferson (Democratic-Republican), 162	Charles C. Pinckney (Federalist), 14
1808	James Madison (Democratic-Republican), 122	Charles C. Pinckney (Federalist), 47
1812	James Madison (Democratic-Republican), 128	DeWitt Clinton (Federalist), 89
1816	James Monroe (Democratic-Republican), 183	Rufus King (Federalist), 34
1820	James Monroe (Democratic-Republican), 231	John Quincy Adams (National-Republican), 1
1824	John Quincy Adams (National-Republican), 84[2]	Andrew Jackson (Democratic-Republican), 99
1828	Andrew Jackson (Democrat), 178	John Quincy Adams (National-Republican), 83
1832	Andrew Jackson (Democrat), 219	Henry Clay (National-Republican), 49
1836	Martin Van Buren (Democrat), 170	William H. Harrison (Whig), 73
1840	William H. Harrison (Whig), 234	Martin Van Buren (Democrat), 60

2. In the 1824 presidential election, no candidate received a majority of electoral votes. Since no candidate received an Electoral College majority, the House of Representatives decided the election. The House chose John Quincy Adams—son of John Adams—to be the nation's next president.

1844	James K. Polk (Democrat), 170	Henry Clay (Whig), 105
1848	Zachary Taylor (Whig), 163	Lewis Cass (Democrat), 127
1852	Franklin Pierce (Democrat), 254	Winfield Scott (Whig), 42
1856	James Buchanan (Democrat), 174	John C. Fremont (Republican), 114
1860	Abraham Lincoln (Republican), 180[3]	John C. Breckinridge (Democrat), 72
1864	Abraham Lincoln (Republican), 212	George B. McClellan (Democrat), 21
1868	Ulysses S. Grant (Republican), 214	Horatio Seymour (Democrat), 80
1872	Ulysses S. Grant (Republican), 286	Horace Greeley (Liberal-Republican, Democrat)–[4]
1876	Rutherford B. Hayes (Republican), 185	Samuel J. Tilden (Democrat), 184
1880	James A. Garfield (Republican), 214	Winfield S. Hancock (Democrat), 155
1884	Grover Cleveland (Democrat), 219	James G. Blaine (Republican), 182
1888	Benjamin Harrison (Republican), 233	Grover Cleveland (Democrat), 168

3. The 1860 election was actually a four-person race, although Abraham Lincoln's main opponent was believed to be Illinois Senator Stephen A. Douglas. Douglas, however, came in fourth place in the Electoral College. John C. Breckinridge came in second, with 72 electoral votes.

4. Horace Greeley died shortly after the 1872 election—before the Electoral College had even met to elect the new president.

1892	Grover Cleveland (Democrat), 277	Benjamin Harrison (Republican), 145
1896	William McKinley (Republican), 271	William Jennings Bryan (Democrat), 176
1900	William McKinley (Republican), 292	William Jennings Bryan (Democrat), 155
1904	Theodore Roosevelt (Republican), 336	Alton B. Parker (Democrat), 140
1908	William H. Taft (Republican), 321	William Jennings Bryan (Democrat), 162
1912	Woodrow Wilson (Democrat), 435	Theodore Roosevelt (Progressive), 88
1916	Woodrow Wilson (Democrat), 277	Charles E. Hughes (Republican), 254
1920	Warren G. Harding (Republican), 404	James M. Cox (Democrat), 127
1924	Calvin Coolige (Republican), 382	John W. Davis (Democrat), 136
1928	Herbert Hoover (Republican), 444	Alfred E. Smith (Democrat), 87
1932	Franklin D. Roosevelt (Democrat), 472	Herbert Hoover (Republican), 59
1936	Franklin D. Roosevelt (Democrat), 523	Alfred Landon (Republican), 8
1940	Franklin D. Roosevelt (Democrat), 449	Wendell Willkie (Republican), 82

1944	Franklin D. Roosevelt (Democrat), 432	Thomas E. Dewey (Republican), 99
1948	Harry S. Truman (Democrat), 303	Thomas E. Dewey (Republican), 189
1952	Dwight D. Eisenhower (Republican), 442	Adlai Stevenson (Democrat), 89
1956	Dwight D. Eisenhower (Republican), 457	Adlai Stevenson (Democrat), 73
1960	John F. Kennedy (Democrat), 303	Richard M. Nixon (Republican), 219
1964	Lyndon B. Johnson (Democrat), 486	Barry Goldwater (Republican), 52
1968[5]	Richard M. Nixon (Republican), 301	Hubert H. Humphrey (Democrat), 191
1972	Richard M. Nixon (Republican), 520	George McGovern (Democrat), 17
1976	Jimmy Carter (Democrat), 297	Gerald Ford (Republican), 240
1980	Ronald Reagan (Republican), 489	Jimmy Carter (Democrat), 49
1984	Ronald Reagan (Republican), 525	Walter Mondale (Democrat), 13
1988	George H. W. Bush (Republican), 426	Michael Dukakis (Democrat), 111

5. Alabama governor and segregationist George Wallace won 46 electoral votes in the 1968 presidential election. He ran under the banner of the American Independent Party.

1992	William Jefferson Clinton (Democrat), 370	George H. W. Bush (Republican), 168
1996	William Jefferson Clinton (Democrat), 379	Bob Dole (Republican), 159
2000	George W. Bush (Republican), 271	Albert Gore Jr. (Democrat), 266
2004	George W. Bush (Republican), 286	John F. Kerry (Democrat), 251
2008	Barack Obama (Democrat), 365	John McCain (Republican), 173

☆ FURTHER READING ☆

Presidential Campaigns, Paul F. Boller Jr. (Oxford University Press, New York, 2004). Brief, readable narratives of every presidential campaign from 1789 through 2000.

The American Presidents, David C. Whitney (Readers Digest, New York, 1996). Brief, informative biographies of all American presidents from George Washington through Bill Clinton.

Presidential Elections: Strategies and Structures of American Politics, Nelson W. Polsby, Steven E. Schier, and David A. Hopkins (Rowman & Littlefield, New York, 2011).

Primary Politics: How Presidential Candidates Have Shaped the Modern Nominating System, Elaine Ciulla Kamarck (Brookings Institution Press, Washington, 2009). An examination on how past candidates and campaigns have shaped our modern presidential nominating system.

Party Politics in America (Longman Classics in Political Science), Marjorie R. Hershey (Longman, 2010). A classic text on U.S. political parties and campaigns.

The Last Campaign, Thurston Clarke. (Henry Holt, New York, 2008). A book about Senator Robert F. Kennedy's presidential campaign in 1968.

Truman, David McCullough. (Simon & Schuster, New York, 1993). A biography of President Harry S. Truman, including his campaign for president in 1948.

Presidential Anecdotes, Paul F. Boller, Jr. (Oxford University Press, New York, 1996). A collection of humorous anecdotes about American presidents. This book was written by the same author as *Presidential Campaigns.*

Adams vs. Jefferson: The Tumultuous Election of 1800, John Ferling (Oxford University Press, New York, 2005). An account of American's first contested presidential election. As this book clearly illustrates, brutal, negative campaigning is nothing new in American politics.

Game Change, John Heilemann and Mark Halperin (Harper, New York, 2010). A rather thrilling and controversial account of the inside story behind the 2008 presidential election—from the epic primary battle between Barack Obama and Hillary Rodham Clinton, to the selection of Sarah Palin as John McCain's running mate.

Too Close to Call: The Thirty-Six-Day Battle to Decide the 2000 Election, Jeffrey Toobin (Random House, New York, 2002). Jeffrey Toobin, a political commentator/journalist and legal analyst, takes an in-depth look at Bush vs. Gore and the contested 2000 presidential election.

Most speeches given during the course of a presidential campaign are not memorable. They have little effect on the campaign, and receive little or no coverage in the press. Occasionally, however, candidates give speeches that—at least temporarily—shake up a the presidential race and change the dynamic of the campaign.

At the 2004 Democratic National Convention, Illinois state senator (and U.S. Senate candidate) Barack Obama gave the keynote address. The speech electrified the audience, and pundits soon began to speculate that America may have just been introduced to its first African American president. Four years, later, Obama appeared before the Democratic National Convention to accept his party's nomination for president—and went on to win the presidency.

Thank you so much. Thank you. Thank you. Thank you so much. Thank you so much. Thank you. Thank you. Thank you, Dick Durbin. You make us all proud. On behalf of the great state of Illinois, crossroads of a nation, Land of Lincoln, let me express my deepest gratitude for the privilege of addressing this convention. Tonight is a particular honor for me because, let's face it, my presence on this stage is pretty unlikely. My father was a foreign student, born and raised in a small village in Kenya. He grew up herding goats, went to school in a tin-roof shack. His father—my grandfather—was a cook, a domestic servant to the British.

But my grandfather had larger dreams for his son. Through hard work and perseverance my father got a scholarship to study in a magical place, America, that shone as a beacon of freedom and opportunity to so many who had come before.

While studying here, my father met my mother. She was born in a town on the other side of the world, in Kansas. Her father worked on oil rigs and farms through most of the Depression. The day after Pearl Harbor my grandfather signed up for duty; joined Patton's army, marched across Europe. Back home, my grandmother raised a baby and went to work on a bomber assembly line. After the war, they studied on the G.I. Bill, bought a house through F.H.A., and later moved west all the way to Hawaii in search of opportunity.

And they, too, had big dreams for their daughter. A common dream, born of two continents.

My parents shared not only an improbable love, they shared an abiding faith in the possibilities of this nation. They would give me an African name, Barack, or "blessed," believing that in a tolerant America your name is no barrier to success. They imagined—They imagined me going to the best schools in the land, even though they weren't rich, because in a generous America you don't have to be rich to achieve your potential.

They're both passed away now. And yet, I know that on this night they look down on me with great pride.

They stand here—And I stand here today, grateful for the diversity of my heritage, aware that my parents' dreams live on in my two precious daughters. I stand here knowing that my story is part of the larger American story, that I owe a debt to all of those who came before me, and that, in no other country on earth, is my story even possible.

Tonight, we gather to affirm the greatness of our Nation—not because of the height of our skyscrapers, or the power of our military, or the size of our economy. Our pride is based on a very simple premise, summed up in a declaration made over two hundred years ago:

We hold these truths to be self-evident, that all men are created equal, that they are endowed by their Creator with certain inalienable rights, that among these are Life, Liberty and the pursuit of Happiness.

That is the true genius of America, a faith—a faith in simple dreams, an insistence on small miracles; that we can tuck in our children at night and know that they are fed and clothed and safe from harm; that we can say what we think, write what we think, without hearing a sudden knock on the door; that we can have an idea and start our own business without paying a bribe; that we can participate in the political process without fear of retribution, and that our votes will be counted—at least most of the time.

This year, in this election we are called to reaffirm our values and our commitments, to hold them against a hard reality and see how we're measuring up to the legacy of our forbearers and the promise of future generations.

And fellow Americans, Democrats, Republicans, Independents, I say to you tonight: We have more work to do—more work to do for the workers I met in Galesburg, Illinois, who are losing their union jobs at the Maytag plant that's moving to Mexico, and now are having to compete with their own children for jobs that pay seven bucks an hour; more to do for the father that I met who was losing his job and choking back the tears, wondering how he would pay 4500 dollars a month for the drugs his son needs without the health benefits that he counted on; more to do for the young woman in East St. Louis, and thousands more like her, who has the grades, has the drive, has the will, but doesn't have the money to go to college.

Now, don't get me wrong. The people I meet—in small towns and big cities, in diners and office parks—they don't expect government to solve all their problems. They know they have to work hard to get ahead, and they want to. Go into the collar counties around Chicago, and people will tell you they don't want their tax money wasted, by a welfare agency or by the Pentagon. Go in—Go into any inner city neighborhood, and folks will tell you that government alone can't teach our kids to learn; they know that parents have to teach, that children can't achieve unless we raise their expectations and turn off the television sets and eradicate the slander that says a black youth with a book is acting white. They know those things.

People don't expect—People don't expect government to solve all their problems. But they sense, deep in their bones, that with just a slight change in priorities, we can make sure that every child in America has a decent shot at life, and that the doors of opportunity remain open to all.

They know we can do better. And they want that choice.

In this election, we offer that choice. Our Party has chosen a man to lead us who embodies the best this country has to offer. And that man is John Kerry.

John Kerry understands the ideals of community, faith, and service because they've defined his life. From his heroic service to Vietnam, to his years as a prosecutor and lieutenant governor, through two decades in the United States Senate, he's devoted himself to this country. Again and again, we've seen him make tough choices when easier ones were available.

His values and his record affirm what is best in us. John Kerry believes in an America where hard work is rewarded; so instead of offering tax breaks to companies shipping jobs overseas, he offers them to companies creating jobs here at home. John Kerry believes in an America where all Americans can afford the same health coverage our politicians in Washington have for themselves.

John Kerry believes in energy independence, so we aren't held hostage to the profits of oil companies, or the sabotage of foreign oil fields.

John Kerry believes in the Constitutional freedoms that have made our country the envy of the world, and he will never sacrifice our basic liberties, nor use faith as a wedge to divide us.

And John Kerry believes that in a dangerous world war must be an option sometimes, but it should never be the first option.

You know, a while back—a while back I met a young man named Shamus in a V.F.W. Hall in East Moline, Illinois. He was a good-looking kid—six two, six three, clear eyed, with an easy smile. He told me he'd joined the Marines and was heading to Iraq the following week. And as I listened to him explain why he'd enlisted, the absolute faith he had in our country and its leaders, his devotion to duty and service, I thought this young man was all that any of us might ever hope for in a child.

But then I asked myself, "Are we serving Shamus as well as he is serving us?" I thought of the 900 men and women—sons and daughters, husbands and wives, friends and neighbors, who won't be returning to their own hometowns. I thought of the families I've met who were struggling to get by without a loved one's full income, or whose loved ones had returned with a limb missing or nerves shattered, but still lacked long-term health benefits because they were Reservists.

When we send our young men and women into harm's way, we have a solemn obligation not to fudge the numbers or shade the truth about why they're going, to care for their families while they're gone, to tend to the soldiers upon their return, and to never ever go to war without enough troops to win the war, secure the peace, and earn the respect of the world.

Now—Now let me be clear. Let me be clear. We have real enemies in the world. These enemies must be found. They must be pursued. And they must be defeated. John Kerry knows this. And just as Lieutenant Kerry did not hesitate to risk his life to protect the men who served with him in Vietnam, President Kerry will not hesitate one moment to use our military might to keep America safe and secure.

John Kerry believes in America. And he knows that

it's not enough for just some of us to prosper—for alongside our famous individualism, there's another ingredient in the American saga, a belief that we're all connected as one people. If there is a child on the south side of Chicago who can't read, that matters to me, even if it's not my child. If there is a senior citizen somewhere who can't pay for their prescription drugs, and having to choose between medicine and the rent, that makes my life poorer, even if it's not my grandparent. If there's an Arab American family being rounded up without benefit of an attorney or due process, that threatens my civil liberties.

It is that fundamental belief—It is that fundamental belief: I am my brother's keeper. I am my sister's keeper that makes this country work. It's what allows us to pursue our individual dreams and yet still come together as one American family. E pluribus unum: "Out of many, one."

Now even as we speak, there are those who are preparing to divide us—the spin masters, the negative ad peddlers who embrace the politics of "anything goes." Well, I say to them tonight, there is not a liberal America and a conservative America—there is the United States of America. There is not a Black America and a White America and Latino America and Asian America—there's the United States of America.

The pundits, the pundits like to slice-and-dice our country into Red States and Blue States; Red States for Republicans, Blue States for Democrats. But I've got news for them, too. We worship an "awesome God" in the Blue States, and we don't like federal agents poking around in our libraries in the Red States. We coach Little League in the Blue States and yes, we've got some gay friends in the Red States. There are patriots who opposed the war in Iraq and there are patriots who supported the war in Iraq. We are one people, all of us pledging allegiance to the stars and stripes, all of us defending the United States of America.

In the end—In the end—In the end, that's what this election is about. Do we participate in a politics of cynicism or do we participate in a politics of hope? John Kerry calls on us to hope. John Edwards calls on us to hope.

I'm not talking about blind optimism here—the almost willful ignorance that thinks unemployment will go away if we just don't think about it, or the health care crisis will solve itself if we just ignore it. That's not what I'm talking about. I'm talking about something more substantial. It's the hope of slaves sitting around a fire singing freedom songs; the hope of immigrants setting out for distant shores; the hope of a young naval lieutenant bravely patrolling the Mekong Delta; the hope of a millworker's son who dares to defy the odds; the hope of a skinny kid with a funny name who believes that America has a place for him, too.

Hope—Hope in the face of difficulty. Hope in the face of uncertainty. The audacity of hope!

In the end, that is God's greatest gift to us, the bedrock of this nation. A belief in things not seen. A belief that there are better days ahead.

I believe that we can give our middle class relief and provide working families with a road to opportunity.

I believe we can provide jobs to the jobless, homes to the homeless, and reclaim young people in cities across America from violence and despair. I believe that we have a righteous wind at our backs and that as we stand on the crossroads of history, we can make the right choices, and meet the challenges that face us.

America! Tonight, if you feel the same energy that I do, if you feel the same urgency that I do, if you feel the same passion that I do, if you feel the same hopefulness that I do—if we do what we must do, then I have no doubt that all across the country, from Florida to Oregon, from Washington to Maine, the people will rise up in November, and John Kerry will be sworn in as President, and John Edwards will be sworn in as Vice President, and this country will reclaim its promise, and out of this long political darkness a brighter day will come.

Thank you very much everybody. God bless you. Thank you.

In the 1952 presidential election, Dwight D. Eisenhower's landslide victory over Adlai Stevenson was, in part, due to his credibility on matters of war and peace. With this speech, Eisenhower sought to convince the nation that he was the candidate who could bring the Korean War to an end.

In this anxious autumn for America, one fact looms above all others in our people's mind. One tragedy challenges all men dedicated to the work of peace. One word shouts denial to those who foolishly pretend that ours is not a nation at war. This fact, this tragedy, this word is: Korea.

A small country, Korea has been, for more than two years, the battleground for the costliest foreign war our nation has fought, excepting the two world wars. It shall been the burial ground for 20,000 America dead. It has been another historic field of honor for the valor and skill and tenacity of American soldiers.

All these things it has been—and yet one thing more. It has been a symbol—a telling symbol—of the foreign policy of our nation.

It has been a sign—a warning sign—of the way the Administration has conducted our world affairs.

It has been a measure—a damning measure—of the quality of leadership we have been given.

Tonight I am going to talk about our foreign policy and of its supreme symbol—the Korean war. I am not going to give you elaborate generalizations—but hard, tough facts. I am going to state the unvarnished truth.

What, then, are the plain facts?

The biggest fact about the Korean war is this: It was never inevitable, it was never inescapable, no fantastic fiat of history decreed that little South Korea—in the summer of 1950—would fatally tempt Communist aggressors as their easiest victim. No demonic destiny decreed that America had to be bled this way in order to keep South Korea free and to keep freedom itself self-respecting.

We are not mute prisoners of history. That is a doctrine for totalitarians, it is no creed for free men.

There is a Korean war—and we are fighting it—for the simplest of reasons: Because free leadership failed to check and to turn back Communist ambition before it savagely attacked us. The Korean war—more perhaps than any other war in history—simply and swiftly followed the collapse of our political defenses. There is no other reason than this: We failed to read and to outwit the totalitarian mind.

I know something of this totalitarian mind. Through

the years of World War II, I carried a heavy burden of decision in the free world's crusade against the tyranny then threatening us all. Month after month, year after year, I had to search out and to weigh the strengths and weaknesses of an enemy driven by the lust to rule the great globe itself.

World War II should have taught us all one lesson. The lesson is this: To vacillate, to hesitate—to appease even by merely betraying unsteady purpose—is to feed a dictator's appetite for conquest and to invite war itself.

That lesson—which should have firmly guided every great decision of our leadership through these later years— was ignored in the development of the Administration's policies for Asia since the end of World War II. Because it was ignored, the record of these policies is a record of appalling failure.

The record of failure dates back—with red-letter folly—at least to September of 1947. It was then that Gen. Albert Wedemeyer—returned from a Presidential mission to the Far East—submitted to the President this warning: "The withdrawal of American military forces from Korea would result in the occupation of South Korea by either Soviet troops or, as seems more likely, by the Korean military units trained under Soviet auspices in North Korea."

That warning and his entire report were disregarded and suppressed by the Administration.

The terrible record of these years reaches its dramatic climax in a series of unforgettable scenes on Capitol Hill in June of 1949. By then the decision to complete withdrawal of American forces from Korea—despite menacing signs from the North—had been drawn up by the

Department of State. The decision included the intention to ask Congress for aid to Korea to compensate for the withdrawal of American forces.

This brought questions from Congress. The Administration parade of civilian and military witnesses before the House Foreign Affairs Committee was headed by the Secretary of State. He and his aides faced a group of Republican Congressmen both skeptical and fearful.

What followed was historic and decisive.

I beg you to listen carefully to the words that followed, for they shaped this nation's course from that date to this. Listen, then:

First: Republican Congressman John Lodge of Connecticut asked "(do) you feel that the Korean Government is able to fill the vacuum caused by the withdrawal of the occupation forces?"

The Administration answered: "Definitely."

Second: A very different estimate of the risk involved came from Republican Congressman Walter Judd of Minnesota. He warned: "I think the thing necessary to give security to Korea at this stage of the game is the presence of a small American force and the knowledge (on the Soviet side) that attack upon it would bring trouble with us."

"I am convinced," Representative Judd continued, "that if we keep even a battalion there, they are not going to move. And if the battalion is not there"—listen now to his warning—"the chances are they will move within a year."

What a tragedy that the Administration shrugged off that accurate warning!

Third: The Secretary of State was asked if he agreed

that the South Koreans alone—and I quote—"will be able to defend themselves against any attack from the northern half of the country." To this the Secretary answered briskly: "We share the same view. Yes, sir."

Rarely in Congressional testimony has so much misinformation been compressed so efficiently into so few words.

Fourth: Republican Congressman Lodge had an incisive comment on all this. "That," he said, "is wishful thinking . . . I am afraid it confesses a kind of fundamental isolationism that exists in certain branches of the Government, which I think is a very dangerous pattern. I think the presence of our troops there is a tremendous deterrent to the Russians."

Finally: This remarkable scene of the summer of 1949 ends with a memorable document. The minority report of five Republican members of the House Foreign Affairs Committee on July 26, 1949, submitted this solemn warning.

Listen to it:

"It is reliably reported that Soviet troops, attached to the North Korean puppet armies, are in position of command as well as acting as advisors . . . This development may well presage the launching of a full-scale military drive across the Thirty-eighth Parallel.

"Our forces . . . have been withdrawn from South Korea at the very instant when logic and common sense both demanded no retreat from the realities of the situation."

The report continues: "Already along the Thirty-eighth Parallel aggression is speaking with the too-familiar voices of howitzers and cannons. Our position is untenable and indefensible.

"The House should be aware of these facts."

These words of eloquent, reasoned warning were spoken eleven months before the Korean war broke.

Behind these words was a fervent, desperate appeal. That appeal was addressed to the Administration. It begged at least some firm statement of American intention that might deter the foreseen attack.

What was the Administration answer to that appeal?

The first answer was silence—stubborn, sullen silence for six months.

Then, suddenly, came speech—a high Government official at long last speaking out on Asia. It was now January of 1950. What did he say? He said, "The United States Government will not provide military aid or advice to Chinese forces on Formosa." Then, one week later, the Secretary of State announced his famous "defense perimeter"—publicly advising our enemies that, so far as nations outside this perimeter were concerned, "no person can guarantee these areas against military attack." Under these circumstances, it was cold comfort to the nations outside this perimeter to be reminded that they could appeal to the United Nations.

These nations, of course, included Korea. The armies of communism, thus informed, began their big build-up. Six months later they were ready to strike across the Thirty-eighth Parallel. They struck on June 25, 1950.

On that day, the record of political and diplomatic failure of this Administration was completed and sealed.

The responsibility for this record cannot be dodged or evaded. Even if not a single Republican leader had warned so clearly against the coming disaster, the responsibility for the fateful political decisions would still rest wholly with the men charged with making those decisions—in the Department of State and in the White House. They cannot escape that responsibility now or ever.

When the enemy struck, on that June day of 1950, what did America do? It did what it always has done in all its times of peril. It appealed to the heroism of its youth. This appeal was utterly right and utterly inescapable. It was inescapable not only because this was the only way to defend the idea of collective freedom against savage aggression. That appeal was inescapable because there was now in the plight into which we had stumbled no other way to save honor and self-respect.

The answer to that appeal has been what any American knew it would be. It has been sheer valor—valor on all the Korean mountainsides that, each day, bear fresh scars of new graves.

Now—in this anxious autumn—from these heroic men there comes back an answering appeal. It is no whine, no whimpering plea. It is a question that addresses itself to simple reason. It asks: Where do we go from here? When comes the end? Is there an end?

These questions touch all of us. They demand truthful answers. Neither glib promises nor glib excuses will serve. They would be no better than the glib prophecies that brought us to this pass.

To these questions there are two false answers—both equally false. The first would be any answer that dishonestly pledged an end to war in Korea by any imminent, exact date. Such a pledge would brand its speaker as a deceiver.

The second and equally false answer declares that nothing can be done to speed a secure peace. It dares to tell us that we, the strongest nation in the history of freedom, can only wait—and wait—and wait. Such a statement brands its speaker as a defeatist.

My answer—candid and complete—is this:

The first task of a new Administration will be to review and re-examine every course of action open to us with one goal in view: To bring the Korean war to an early and honorable end. This is my pledge to the American people.

For this task a wholly new Administration is necessary. The reason for this is simple. The old Administration cannot be expected to repair what it failed to prevent.

Where will a new Administration begin?

It will begin with its President taking a simple, firm resolution. The resolution will be: To forego the diversions of politics and to concentrate on the job of ending the Korean war—until that job is honorably done.

That job requires a personal trip to Korea.

I shall make that trip. Only in that way could I learn how best to serve the American people in the cause of peace.

I shall go to Korea.

That is my second pledge to the American people.

Carefully, then, this new Administration, unfettered by past decisions and inherited mistakes, can review every factor—military, political and psychological—to be mobilized in speeding a just peace.

Progress along at least two lines can instantly begin. We can—first—step up the program of training and arming the South Korean forces. Manifestly, under the circumstances of today, United Nations forces cannot abandon that unhappy land. But just as troops of the

Republic of Korea covet and deserve the honor of defending their frontiers, so should we give them maximum assistance to insure their ability to do so.

Then, United Nations forces in reserve positions and supporting roles would be assurance that disaster would not again strike.

We can—secondly—shape our psychological warfare program into a weapon capable of cracking the Communist front.

Beyond all this we must carefully weigh all interrelated courses of action. We will, of course, constantly confer with associated free nations of Asia and with the cooperating members of the United Nations. Thus we could bring into being a practical plan for world peace.

That is my third pledge to you.

As the next Administration goes to work for peace, we must be guided at every instant by that lesson I spoke of earlier. The vital lesson is this: To vacillate, to appease, to placate is only to invite war—vaster war—bloodier war. In the words of the late Senator [Arthur H.] Vandenberg, appeasement is not the road to peace; it is only surrender on the installment plan.

I will always reject appeasement.

And that is my fourth pledge to you.

A nation's foreign policy is a much graver matter than rustling papers and bustling conferences. It is much more than diplomatic decisions and trade treaties and military arrangements.

A foreign policy is the face and voice of a whole people. It is all that the world sees and hears and understands about a single nation. It expresses the character and the faith and the will of that nation. In this, a nation is like any individual of our personal acquaintance; the simplest gesture can betray hesitation or weakness, the merest inflection of voice can reveal doubt or fear.

It is in this deep sense that our foreign policy has faltered and failed.

For a democracy, a great election, such as this, signifies a most solemn trial. It is the time when—to the bewilderment of all tyrants—the people sit in judgment upon the leaders. It is the time when these leaders are summoned before the bar of public decision. There they must give evidence both to justify their actions and explain their intentions.

In the great trial of this election, the judges—the people—must not be deceived into believing that the choice is between isolationism and internationalism. That is a debate of the dead past. The vast majority of Americans of both parties know that to keep their own nation free, they bear a majestic responsibility for freedom through all the world. As practical people, Americans also know the critical necessity of unimpaired access to raw materials on other continents for our own economic and military strength.

Today the choice—the real choice—lies between policies that assume that responsibility awkwardly and fearfully—and policies that accept that responsibility with sure purpose and firm will. The choice is between foresight and blindness, between doing and apologizing, between planning and improvising.

In rendering their verdict, the people must judge with courage and with wisdom. For—at this date— any faltering in America's leadership is a capital offense against freedom.

In this trial, my testimony, of a personal kind, is quite simple. A soldier all my life, I have enlisted in the greatest cause of my life—the cause of peace.

I do not believe it a presumption for me to call the effort of all who have enlisted with me—a crusade.

I use that word only to signify two facts. First: We are united and devoted to a just cause of the purest meaning to all humankind. Second: We know that—for all the might of our effort—victory can come only with the gift of God's help.

In this spirit—humble servants of a proud ideal—we do soberly say: This is a crusade.

At the 1948 Democratic National Convention, Minneapolis Mayor (and future U.S. senator and vice president) Hubert Humphrey made an urgent, passionate appeal to the conscience of the Democratic Party. He urged convention delegates to reject segregation and embrace civil rights.

Mr. Chairman, fellow Democrats, fellow Americans:

I realize that in speaking in behalf of the minority report on civil rights as presented by Congressman DeMiller of Wisconsin that I'm dealing with a charged issue—with an issue which has been confused by emotionalism on all sides of the fence. I realize that there are here today friends and colleagues of mine, many of them, who feel just as deeply and keenly as I do about this issue and who are yet in complete disagreement with me.

My respect and admiration for these men and their views was great when I came to this convention. It is now far greater because of the sincerity, the courtesy, and the forthrightness with which many of them have argued in our prolonged discussions in the platform committee.

Because of this very great respect—and because of my profound belief that we have a challenging task to do here—because good conscience, decent morality, demands it—I feel I must rise at this time to support a report—the minority report—a report that spells out our democracy, a report that the people of this country can and will understand, and a report that they will enthusiastically acclaim on the great issue of civil rights.

Now let me say this at the outset that this proposal is made for no single region. Our proposal is made for no single class, for no single racial or religious group in mind. All of the regions of this country, all of the states have shared in our precious heritage of American freedom. All the states and all the regions have seen at least some of the infringements of that freedom—all people— get this—all people, white and black, all groups, all racial groups have been the victims at time[s] in this nation of—let me say—vicious discrimination.

The masterly statement of our keynote speaker, the distinguished United States Senator from Kentucky, Alben Barkley, made that point with great force. Speaking of the founder of our Party, Thomas Jefferson, he said this, and I quote from Alben Barkley:

He did not proclaim that all the white, or the black, or the red, or the yellow men are equal; that all Christian or Jewish men are equal; that all Protestant and Catholic men are equal; that all rich and poor men are equal; that all good and bad men are equal. What he declared was that all men are equal; and the equality which he proclaimed was the equality in the right to enjoy the blessings of free government in which they may participate and to which they have given their support.

Now these words of Senator Barkley's are appropriate to this convention—appropriate to this convention of the oldest, the most truly progressive political party in America. From the time of Thomas Jefferson, the time when that immortal American doctrine of individual rights, under just and fairly administered laws, the Democratic Party has tried hard to secure expanding freedoms for all citizens. Oh, yes, I know, other political parties may have talked more about civil rights, but the Democratic party has surely done more about civil rights.

We have made progress—we've made great progress in every part of this country. We've made great progress in the South; we've made it in the West, in the North, and in the East. But we must now focus the direction of that progress towards the—towards the realization of a full program of civil rights to all. This convention must set out more specifically the direction in which our Party efforts are to go. We can be proud that we can be guided by the courageous trail blazing of two great Democratic Presidents. We can be proud of the fact that our great and beloved immortal leader Franklin Roosevelt gave us guidance. And we be proud of the fact—we can be proud of the fact that Harry Truman has had the courage to give to the people of America the new emancipation proclamation.

It seems to me—It seems to me that the Democratic Party needs to to make definite pledges of the kinds suggested in the minority report, to maintain the trust and the confidence placed in it by the people of all races and all sections of this country. Sure, we're here as Democrats. But my good friends, we're here as Americans; we're here as the believers in the principle and the ideology of democracy, and I firmly believe that as men concerned with our country's future, we must specify in our platform the guarantees which we have mentioned in the minority report.

Yes, this is far more than a Party matter. Every citizen in this country has a stake in the emergence of the United States as a leader in the free world. That world is being challenged by the world of slavery. For us to play our part effectively, we must be in a morally sound position.

We can't use a double standard—There's no room for double standards in American politics—for measuring our own and other people's policies. Our demands for democratic practices in other lands will be no more effective than the guarantee of those practices in our own country.

Friends, delegates, I do not believe that there can be any compromise on the guarantees of the civil rights which we have mentioned in the minority report. In spite of my desire for unanimous agreement on the entire platform, in spite of my desire to see everybody here in honest and unanimous agreement, there are some matters which I think must be stated clearly and without qualification. There can be no hedging—the newspaper headlines are wrong. There will be no hedging, and there will be no watering down—if you please—of the instruments and the principles of the civil-rights program.

My friends, to those who say that we are rushing this issue of civil rights, I say to them we are 172 years late. To those who say that this civil-rights program is an infringement on states' rights, I say this: The time has arrived in America for the Democratic Party to get out of the shadow of states' rights and to walk forthrightly into the bright sunshine of human rights. People—human beings—this is the issue of the 20th century. People of all kinds—all sorts of people—and these people are looking to America for leadership, and they're looking to America for precept and example.

My good friends, my fellow Democrats, I ask you for a calm consideration of our historic opportunity. Let us do forget the evil passions and the blindness of the past. In these times of world economic, political, and spiritual— above all spiritual crisis, we cannot and we must not turn from the path so plainly before us. That path has already lead us through many valleys of the shadow of death. And now is the time to recall those who were left on that path of American freedom.

For all of us here, for the millions who have sent us, for the whole two billion members of the human family, our land is now, more than ever before, the last best hope on earth. And I know that we can, and I know that we shall began [sic] here the fuller and richer realization of that hope, that promise of a land where all men are truly free and equal, and each man uses his freedom and equality wisely well.

My good friends, I ask my Party, I ask the Democratic Party, to march down the high road of progressive democracy. I ask this convention to say in unmistakable terms that we proudly hail, and we courageously support, our President and leader Harry Truman in his great fight for civil rights in America!

Senator Barry Goldwater (R-AZ)'s acceptance speech at the 1964 Republican National Convention was widely viewed as a political disaster, having aided Democratic efforts to portray him as a dangerous extremist. While Goldwater lost in a landslide to Lyndon B. Johnson, his convention speech inspired a new generation of conservatives, many of whom viewed the Arizona Republican as their hero.

My good friend and great Republican, Dick Nixon, and your charming wife, Pat; my running mate, that wonderful Republican who has served us so well for so long, Bill Miller and his wife, Stephanie; to Thurston Morton who's done such a commendable job in chairmaning this Convention; to Mr. Herbert Hoover, who I hope is watching; and to that—that great American and his wife, General and Mrs. Eisenhower; to my own wife, my family, and to all of my fellow Republicans here assembled, and Americans across this great Nation.

From this moment, united and determined, we will go forward together, dedicated to the ultimate and undeniable greatness of the whole man. Together—Together we will win.

I accept your nomination with a deep sense of humility. I accept, too, the responsibility that goes with it, and I seek your continued help and your continued guidance. My fellow Republicans, our cause is too great for any man to feel worthy of it. Our task would be too great for any man, did he not have with him the hearts and the hands of this great Republican Party, and I promise you tonight that every fiber of my being is consecrated to our cause; that nothing shall be lacking from the struggle that can be brought to it by enthusiasm, by devotion, and plain hard work. In this world no person, no Party can guarantee anything, but what we can do and what we shall do is to deserve victory, and victory will be ours.

The good Lord raised this mighty Republic to be a home for the brave and to flourish as the land of the free—not to stagnate in the swampland of collectivism, not to cringe before the bullying of communism.

Now, my fellow Americans, the tide has been running against freedom. Our people have followed false prophets. We must, and we shall, return to proven ways—not because they are old, but because they are true. We must, and we shall, set the tides running again in the cause of freedom. And this party, with its every action, every word, every breath, and every heartbeat, has but a single resolve, and that is freedom—freedom made orderly for this Nation by our constitutional government; freedom under a government limited by the laws of nature and of nature's God; freedom balanced so that order lacking liberty will not become the slavery of the prison cell; balanced so that liberty lacking order will not become the license of the mob and of the jungle.

Now, we Americans understand freedom. We have earned it; we have lived for it, and we have died for it. This Nation and its people are freedom's model in a searching world. We can be freedom's missionaries in a doubting world. But, ladies and gentlemen, first we must renew freedom's mission in our own hearts and in our own homes.

During four futile years, the administration which we shall replace has—has distorted and lost that vision. It has talked and talked and talked and talked the words of freedom, but it has failed and failed and failed in the works of freedom.

Now, failures cement the wall of shame in Berlin. Failures blot the sands of shame at the Bay of Pigs. Failures mark the slow death of freedom in Laos. Failures infest the jungles of Vietnam. And failures haunt the houses of our once great alliances and undermine the greatest bulwark ever erected by free nations—the NATO community. Failures proclaim lost leadership, obscure purpose, weakening will, and the risk of inciting our sworn enemies to new aggressions and to new excesses.

And because of this administration we are tonight a world divided; we are a Nation becalmed. We have lost the brisk pace of diversity and the genius of individual creativity. We are plodding along at a pace set by centralized planning, red tape, rules without responsibility, and regimentation without recourse.

Rather than useful jobs in our country, our people have been offered bureaucratic "make work"; rather than moral leadership, they have been given bread and circuses. They have been given spectacles, and, yes, they've even been given scandals.

Tonight, there is violence in our streets, corruption in our highest offices, aimlessness amongst our youth, anxiety among our elders, and there's a virtual despair among the many who look beyond material success for the inner meaning of their lives. And where examples of morality should be set, the opposite is seen. Small men, seeking great wealth or power, have too often and too long turned even the highest levels of public service into mere personal opportunity.

Now, certainly, simple honesty is not too much to demand of men in government. We find it in most. Republicans demand it from everyone. They demand it from everyone no matter how exalted or protected his position might be. Now the—the growing menace in our country tonight, to personal safety, to life, to limb and property, in homes, in churches, on the playgrounds, and places of business, particularly in our great cities, is the mounting concern, or should be, of every thoughtful citizen in the United States.

Security from domestic violence, no less than from foreign aggression, is the most elementary and fundamental purpose of any government, and a government that cannot fulfill this purpose is one that cannot long command the loyalty of its citizens.

History shows us—it demonstrates that nothing, nothing prepares the way for tyranny more than the failure of public officials to keep the streets safe from bullies and marauders.

Now, we Republicans see all this as more, much more, than the result of mere political differences or mere political mistakes. We see this as the result of a fundamentally and absolutely wrong view of man, his nature, and his destiny. Those who seek to live your lives for you, to take your liberties in return for relieving you of yours, those who elevate the state and downgrade the citizen must see ultimately a world in which earthly power can be substituted for Divine Will, and this Nation was founded upon the rejection of that notion and upon the acceptance of God as the author of freedom.

Now those who seek absolute power, even though they seek it to do what they regard as good, are simply demanding the right to enforce their own version of heaven on earth. They—and let me remind you, they are the very ones who always create the most hellish tyrannies. Absolute power does corrupt, and those who seek it must be suspect and must be opposed. Their mistaken course stems from false notions, ladies and gentlemen, of equality. Equality, rightly understood, as our founding fathers understood it, leads to liberty and to the emancipation of creative differences. Wrongly understood, as it has been so tragically in our time, it leads first to conformity and then to despotism.

Fellow Republicans, it is the cause of Republicanism to resist concentrations of power, private or public, which—which enforce such conformity and inflict such despotism. It is the cause of Republicanism to ensure that power remains in the hands of the people. And, so help us God, that is exactly what a Republican President will do with the help of a Republican Congress.

It is further the cause of Republicanism to restore a clear understanding of the tyranny of man over man in the world at large. It is our cause to dispel the foggy thinking which avoids hard decisions in the delusion that a world of conflict will somehow mysteriously resolve itself into a world of harmony, if we just don't rock the boat or irritate the forces of aggression—and this is hogwash.

It is further the cause of Republicanism to remind ourselves, and the world, that only the strong can remain free, that only the strong can keep the peace. Now, I needn't remind you, or my fellow Americans regardless of party, that Republicans have shouldered this hard responsibility and marched in this cause before. It was Republican leadership under Dwight Eisenhower that kept the peace, and passed along to this administration the mightiest arsenal for defense the world has ever known. And I needn't remind you that it was the strength and the [un]believable will of the Eisenhower years that kept the peace by using our strength, by using it in the Formosa Straits and in Lebanon and by showing it courageously at all times.

It was during those Republican years that the thrust of Communist imperialism was blunted. It was during those years of Republican leadership that this world moved closer, not to war, but closer to peace, than at any other time in the last three decades.

And I needn't remind you—but I will—that it's been during Democratic years that our strength to deter war has stood still, and even gone into a planned decline. It has been during Democratic years that we have weakly stumbled into conflict, timidly refusing to draw our own lines against aggression, deceitfully refusing to tell even our people of our full participation, and tragically, letting our finest men die on battlefields, unmarked by purpose, unmarked by pride or the prospect of victory. Yesterday, it was Korea. Tonight, it is Vietnam. Make no bones of this. Don't try to sweep this under the rug. We are at war in Vietnam. And yet the President, who is the Commander-in-Chief of our forces, refuses to say—refuses to say, mind you, whether or not the objective over there is victory.

And his Secretary of Defense continues to mislead and misinform the American people, and enough of it has gone by.

And I needn't remind you—but I will—it has been during Democratic years that a billion persons were cast into Communist captivity and their fate cynically sealed. Today—Today in our beloved country we have an administration which seems eager to deal with communism in every coin known—from gold to wheat, from consulates to confidences, and even human freedom itself.

Now the Republican cause demands that we brand communism as the principal disturber of peace in the world today. Indeed, we should brand it as the only significant disturber of the peace, and we must make clear that until its goals of conquest are absolutely renounced and its relations with all nations tempered, communism and the governments it now controls are enemies of every man on earth who is or wants to be free.

Now, we here in America can keep the peace only if we remain vigilant and only if we remain strong. Only if we keep our eyes open and keep our guard up can we prevent war. And I want to make this abundantly clear: I don't intend to let peace or freedom be torn from our grasp because of lack of strength or lack of will—and that I promise you, Americans.

I believe that we must look beyond the defense of freedom today to its extension tomorrow. I believe that the communism which boasts it will bury us will, instead, give way to the forces of freedom. And I can see in the distant and yet recognizable future the outlines of a world worthy of our dedication, our every risk, our every effort, our every sacrifice along the way. Yes, a world that will redeem the suffering of those who will be liberated from tyranny. I can see—and I suggest that all thoughtful men must contemplate—the flowering of an Atlantic civilization, the whole of Europe reunified and freed, trading openly across its borders, communicating openly across the world.

Now, this is a goal far, far more meaningful than a moon shot. It's a—It's a truly inspiring goal for all free men to set for themselves during the latter half of the twentieth century.

I can also see—and all free men must thrill to—the events of this Atlantic civilization joined by its great ocean highway to the United States. What a destiny! What a destiny can be ours to stand as a great central pillar linking Europe, the Americas, and the venerable and vital peoples and cultures of the Pacific. I can see a day when all the Americas, North and South, will be linked in a mighty system, a system in which the errors and misunderstandings of the past will be submerged one by one in a rising tide of prosperity and interdependence. We know that the misunderstandings of centuries are not to be wiped away in a day or wiped away in an hour. But we pledge, we pledge that human sympathy—what our neighbors to the South call an attitude of "simpatico"—no less than enlightened self-interest will be our guide.

And I can see this Atlantic civilization galvanizing and guiding emergent nations everywhere.

Now I know this freedom is not the fruit of every soil. I know that our own freedom was achieved through centuries, by unremitting efforts of brave and wise men. And I know that the road to freedom is a long and a challenging road. And I know also that some men may walk away from it, that some men resist challenge, accepting the false security of governmental paternalism.

And I—And I pledge that the America I envision in the years ahead will extend its hand in health, in teaching and in cultivation, so that all new nations will be at least encouraged—encouraged!—to go our way, so that they will not wander down the dark alleys of tyranny or the dead-end streets of collectivism.

My fellow Republicans, we do no man a service by hiding freedom's light under a bushel of mistaken humility.

I seek an America proud of its past, proud of its ways, proud of its dreams, and determined actively to proclaim them. But our example to the world must, like charity, begin at home.

In our vision of a good and decent future, free and peaceful, there must be room, room for deliberation of the energy and the talent of the individual; otherwise our vision is blind at the outset.

We must assure a society here which, while never abandoning the needy or forsaking the helpless, nurtures incentives and opportunities for the creative and the productive. We must know the whole good is the product of many single contributions.

And I cherish a day when our children once again will restore as heroes the sort of men and women who, unafraid and undaunted, pursue the truth, strive to cure disease, subdue and make fruitful our natural environment and produce the inventive engines of production, science, and technology.

This Nation, whose creative people have enhanced this entire span of history, should again thrive upon the greatness of all those things which we, we as individual citizens, can and should do. And during Republican years, this again will be a nation of men and women, of families proud of their role, jealous of their responsibilities, unlimited in their aspirations—a Nation where all who can will be self-reliant. We Republicans see in our constitutional form of government the great framework which assures the orderly but dynamic fulfillment of the whole man, and we see the whole man as the great reason for instituting orderly government in the first place. We see—We see in private property and in economy based upon and fostering private property, the one way to make government a durable ally of the whole man, rather than his determined enemy. We see in the sanctity of private property the only durable foundation for constitutional government in a free society. And—And beyond that, we see, in cherished diversity of ways, diversity of thoughts, of motives and accomplishments. We don't seek to lead anyone's life for him. We only seek—only seek to secure his rights, guarantee him opportunity—guarantee him opportunity to strive, with government performing only those needed and constitutionally sanctioned tasks which cannot otherwise be performed.

We Republicans seek a government that attends to its inherent responsibilities of maintaining a stable monetary and fiscal climate, encouraging a free and a competitive economy and enforcing law and order. Thus, do we seek inventiveness, diversity, and creative difference within a stable order, for we Republicans define government's role where needed at many, many levels—preferably, though, the one closest to the people involved.

Our towns and our cities, then our counties, then our

states, then our regional compacts—and only then, the national government. That, let me remind you, is the ladder of liberty, built by decentralized power. On it also we must have balance between the branches of government at every level.

Balance, diversity, creative difference: These are the elements of the Republican equation. Republicans agree— Republicans agree heartily to disagree on many, many of their applications, but we have never disagreed on the basic fundamental issues of why you and I are Republicans.

This is a Party. This Republican Party is a Party for free men, not for blind followers, and not for conformists.

In fact, in 1858 Abraham Lincoln said this of the Republican party—and I quote him, because he probably could have said it during the last week or so: "It was composed of strange, discordant, and even hostile elements"—end of the quote—in 1858. Yet—Yet all of these elements agreed on one paramount objective: To arrest the progress of slavery, and place it in the course of ultimate extinction. Today, as then, but more urgently and more broadly than then, the task of preserving and enlarging freedom at home and of safeguarding it from the forces of tyranny abroad is great enough to challenge all our resources and to require all our strength.

Anyone who joins us in all sincerity, we welcome. Those who do not care for our cause, we don't expect to enter our ranks in any case. And—And let our Republicanism, so focused and so dedicated, not be made fuzzy and futile by unthinking and stupid labels.

I would remind you that extremism in the defense of liberty is no vice. And let me remind you also that moderation in the pursuit of justice is no virtue. Why the beauty of the very system we Republicans are pledged to restore and revitalize, the beauty of this Federal system of ours is in its reconciliation of diversity with unity. We must not see malice in honest differences of opinion, and no matter how great, so long as they are not inconsistent with the pledges we have given to each other in and through our Constitution.

Our Republican cause is not to level out the world or make its people conform in computer regimented sameness. Our Republican cause is to free our people and light the way for liberty throughout the world.

Ours is a very human cause for very humane goals.

This Party, its good people, and its unquenchable devotion to freedom, will not fulfill the purposes of this campaign, which we launch here and now, until our cause has won the day, inspired the world, and shown the way to a tomorrow worthy of all our yesteryears.

I repeat, I accept your nomination with humbleness, with pride, and you and I are going to fight for the goodness of our land.

Thank you.

☆ NOTES ☆

2. THE PRIMARIES

1. Kerry Wins Iowa Caucuses, Edwards 3rd, Gephardt to Drop Out: http://articles.cnn.com/2004-01-19/politics/elec04.prez .main_1_caucuses-gephardt-iowa-democratic-party? _s=PM:ALLPOLITICS.

2. Obama Takes Delegate Lead: http://www.politico.com/news/ stories/0208/8358.html.

3. McCain Wins NH: http://articles.cnn.com/2008-01-08/ politics/nh.main_1_democratic-primary-voters-mike-huckabee -new-hampshire?_s=PM:POLITICS.

4. Delegate Count for All Primaries: http://www.cnn.com/ ELECTION/2008/primaries/results/dates/#val=20080205.

5. Democrats and Proportional Representation: http://www .pollingreport.com/delegates.htm.

6. Super Tuesday 2000: http://articles.cnn.com/2000-03-08/ politics/super.tuesday_1_democratic-national-convention-gore -john-mccain-super-tuesday-victories?_s=PM:ALLPOLITICS.

7. Super Tuesday 2008: http://www.cbsnews.com/stories/2008/02/05/politics/main3794580.shtml.

8. Chuck Todd on Obama's Upset. This is the greatest political upset maybe in the history of American politics: http://www.huffingtonpost.com/2008/06/03/obama-wins-democratic-nom_n_105034.html.

9. Dean Elected DNC Chair: http://www.msnbc.msn.com/id/6958538/ns/politics/t/howard-dean-elected-lead-democrats/.

10. Dean vs. Emanuel: http://www.time.com/time/nation/article/0,8599,1483983,00.html.

11. Steele Elected RNC Chair, Defeats Dawson: http://thecaucus.blogs.nytimes.com/2009/01/30/gop-balloting-begins-inconclusively/.

12. DNC Strips Michigan, Florida's Delegates: http://www.theatlantic.com/politics/archive/2007/12/the-dnc-strips-michigan-of-delegates/51150/.

13. James Garfield: http://artandhistory.house.gov/highlights.aspx?action=view&intID=141.

14. House Members Who Eventually Became President: http://artandhistory.house.gov/mem_bio/mem_pres.aspx.

15. Wes Clark Won Oklahoma: http://articles.cnn.com/2004-02-03/politics/elec04.prez.clark_1_wesley-clark-results-tight-race?_s=PM:ALLPOLITICS.

3. THE CONVENTIONS: CLINCHING THE NOMINATION

1. Superdelegates/1984, Mondale vs. Hart: http://www.brook ings.edu/opinions/2008/0215_elections_mann.aspx.

2. Humphrey Speech to 1948 Convention: http://www.mnhs .org/library/tips/history_topics/42humphreyspeech/transcript .htm.

3. African American Vote for President 2000–2008: http:// thecaucus.blogs.nytimes.com/2008/03/20/democrats-in-black -and-white/.

4. 2008 Democratic Platform: http://www.democrats.org/about/ party_platform.

5. 2008 GOP Platform: http://www.gop.com/2008Platform/ Values.htm#1.

6. Stevenson Allows Delegates to Choose Veep: http://www .lib.unc.edu/blogs/morton/index.php/2010/11/a-spark-of -greatness/.

7. Running Mates Were Chosen at Conventions Before 1980s: http://articles.cnn.com/2008-07-30/politics/dem.veepstakes _1_obama-veepstakes-wtop-radio-democratic-convention? _s=PM:POLITICS.

8. Dick Cheney/VP Selection: http://www.bartongellman.com/ angler/fresh-air.php.

9. Biden Campaigns in PA, OH, FL: http://www.politico.com/news/stories/1108/15205.html.

10. Biden on the Campaign Trail (Mark Leibovich piece): http://www.nytimes.com/2008/09/20/us/politics/20biden.html.

11. Hillary Clinton Suspends Roll Call: http://www.nytimes.com/2008/08/28/us/politics/28DEMSDAY.html?pagewanted=2.

12. Obama's Acceptance Speech: http://www.nytimes.com/2008/08/28/us/politics/28text-obama.html.

13. Clinton's Acceptance Speech: http://www.presidency.ucsb.edu/ws/index.php?pid=25958#axzz1MTSyd0t1.

14. Reagan's Acceptance Speech: http://www.presidency.ucsb.edu/ws/index.php?pid=25970#axzz1MTSyd0t1.

15. LBJ's Acceptance Speech: http://www.lbjlib.utexas.edu/johnson/archives.hom/speeches.hom/640827.asp.

16. Eisenhower's Acceptance Speech: http://www.presidency.ucsb.edu/ws/index.php?pid=75626#axzz1MTSyd0t1.

17. McGovern-Fraser: http://www.boston.com/news/globe/ideas/articles/2003/11/23/primary_colors/http://www.senate.gov/reference/resources/pdf/RL30527.pdf. pp. 7–8 of CRS report.

18. Hunt Commission/Superdelegates: http://belfercenter.ksg.harvard.edu/publication/18072/history_of_superdelegates_in_the_democratic_party.html.

4. THE GENERAL ELECTION

1. NY Loses Two House Seats: http://online.wsj.com/article/SB10001424052748703581204576033951298355540.html.

2. Texas Gains Four House Seats: http://voices.washingtonpost.com/thefix/redistricting/red-states-gain-as-new-congres.html.

3. New 2012 Electoral Map: http://www.nytimes.com/interactive/2010/12/21/us/census-districts.html3?ref=us.

4. 2000 Election/Florida Timeline of Events: http://articles.cnn.com/2000-12-13/politics/got.here_1_al-gore-george-w-bush-election-day/5?_s=PM:ALLPOLITICS.

5. 2000 Election Florida Results: http://www.archives.gov/federal-register/electoral-college/2000/popular_vote.html.

6. Dewey Defeats Truman: http://www.chicagotribune.com/news/politics/chi-chicagodays-deweydefeats-story,0,6484067.story.

7. McCullough, David. *Truman*. pp. 703–17.

8. NYT on Swift Boat Vet Claims, and Ties to Bush Campaign: http://www.nytimes.com/2004/08/20/politics/campaign/20swift.html?ex=1250913600&en=9b6f27de16c97265&ei=5090&partner=rssuserland&pagewanted=1.

9. Kerry Files FEC Complaint Against Swift Boat 527: http://articles.cnn.com/2004-08-20/politics/kerry.swiftboat_1_media

-fund-bush-campaign-swift-boat-veterans?_s=PM:ALL
POLITICS.

10. Bush Sues to Stop Liberal 527s: http://www.washington
post.com/wp-dyn/articles/A54455-2004Sep1.html.

11. Mark Penn on Negative Ads: http://www.politico.com/news/
stories/0808/12455.html.

12. George Allen/Macaca: http://voices.washingtonpost.com/
thefix/morning-fix/george-allen-to-run-for-senate.html;
http://www.washingtonpost.com/wp-dyn/content/article/
2006/08/14/AR2006081400589.html

13. Rove Suspected Gore Spokesman in DUI Leak: http://
www.politico.com/news/stories/0310/33946.html.

14. Reagan: "Tear Down This Wall": http://www.american
rhetoric.com/speeches/ronaldreaganbrandenburggate.htm.

15. Bush Defeated Dukakis: http://uselectionatlas.org/
RESULTS/national.php?f=0&year=1988.

16. Dukakis Interview/Tank: http://www.usnews.com/news/
politics/articles/2008/01/17/the-photo-op-that-tanked.

17. Bush Reelected Despite Low Approval Ratings: http://www
.gallup.com/poll/12175/bushs-reelection-prospects-unclear-from
-historical-view.aspx.

18. Gore: I Am My Own Man: http://query.nytimes.com/gst/

fullpage.html?res=9E02E0DB153EF93BA2575BC0A9669
C8B63&pagewanted=2.

19. McCain: I'm Not President Bush: http://articles.cnn.com/
2008-10-15/politics/presidential.debate_1_mccain-illinois
-senator-obama?_s=PM:POLITICS.

20. 1984 Unemployment Rate: http://www.nationaljournal
.com/columns/off-to-the-races/indications-for-2012-20110208
?print=true.

21. Polls Showed Bush with Advantage on Terrorism/Ef-
fects of Bin Ladin Tape: http://abcnews.go.com/sections/us/
politics/bush_kerry_poll_040308.html; http://people-press.
org/2004/08/12/public-faults-bush-on-economy-55-say
-jobs-are-scarce/; http://www.time.com/time/election2004/
article/0,18471,695528,00.html.

Bin Laden Tape/2004 Election: http://legacy.signonsandiego
.com/news/nation/terror/20041029-1423-binladentape.html.

Bush Takes Lead in Polls Following Bin Laden Tape:
http://www.telegraph.co.uk/news/worldnews/northamerica/
usa/1475515/Bush-takes-a-six-point-lead-after-new-bin
-Laden-tape.html.

Kerry Believes Bin Laden Tape Helped Bush: http://www
.nytimes.com/2005/01/31/politics/31kerry.html.

22. Bush/Kerry Debate Negotiations: http://www.time.com/
time/election2004/article/0,18471,702075,00.html.

23. Kennedy/Nixon Debate: http://www.museum.tv/eotvsec
tion.php?entrycode=kennedy-nixon.

24. Bush Checks His Watch: http://www.pbs.org/newshour/debatingourdestiny/dod/1992-broadcast.html.

25. McCain First Debate Performance: http://nationaljournal.com/njonline/insiders-see-an-obama-win-in-first-debate-20080929?mrefid=site_search.

26. McCain Team Reacts to Obama Charge That He Is "losing his bearings": http://www.reuters.com/article/2008/05/09/us-usa-politics-age-idUSN0842591620080509.

27. Late-night Comedy Picks Up McCain Wandering Around Debate Stage: http://www.huffingtonpost.com/2008/10/10/the-mccain-wander_n_133775.html.

28. Gore Approaches Bush During Townhall Debate in 2000: http://community.seattletimes.nwsource.com/archive/?date=20001020&slug=TTK820OL6.

29. Research 2000 Polling Controversy: http://www.politico.com/news/stories/0710/39497.html; http://www.pollster.com/blogs/the_dailykos_research_2000_con.php?nr=1.

30. Presidential Election: Popular Vote Totals: http://www.ropercenter.uconn.edu/elections/common/pop_vote.html.

31. Independent Voters Swung to Obama During Financial Crisis: http://online.wsj.com/article/SB122332442918808789.html.

32. Adams vs. Jefferson Negative Attacks: http://articles.cnn.com/2008-08-22/living/mf.campaign.slurs.slogans_1_jefferson-family-sally-hemings-vice-president-jefferson?

_s=PM:LIVING; McCullough, David. *John Adams*. p. 537; Crawford, Allen Pell. *Twilight at Monticello: The Final Years of Thomas Jefferson*. p. 83.

33. William Henry Harrison Slogans: http://www.nps.gov/nr/ twhp/wwwlps/lessons/4logcabins/4facts3.htm.

34. William Jennings Bryan Rail Speeches 1896: http://proj ects.vassar.edu/1896/bryan.html.

35. Obama Online Fund-Raising: http://voices.washington post.com/44/2008/11/20/obama_raised_half_a_billion_on. html; http://www.pbs.org/newshour/vote2008/reportersblog/ 2008/12/obama_campaign_fundraising_tot.html.

36. Voting Age Population Model vs. Voting Eligible Population Model: http://www.ou.edu/policom/1501_2005_winter/com mentary.htm.

37. 2004 Turnout vs. 2008 Turnout, New Registration vs. New Voters: http://i2.cdn.turner.com/cnn/2008/images/11/06/pdf .gansre08turnout.au.pdf.

38. Voter Turnout in Presidential Elections: http://elections. gmu.edu/Turnout_2008G.html; http://www.presidency.ucsb .edu/data/turnout.php.

39. Norman Hsu/Bundler: http://www.nytimes.com/2007/08/ 31/us/politics/31hsu.html.

40. Perot Led in the Polls: http://www.time.com/time/maga zine/article/0,9171,975880,00.html.

5. ELECTION DAY

1. Exit Polls Showed Kerry Victory in 2004: http://www.wash
ingtonpost.com/wp-dyn/articles/A22188-2005Jan19.html.

2. Shrum Congratulates "President" Kerry: Shrum, Bob. *No
Excuses: Confessions of a Serial Campaigner.* pp. xi–xiv.

3. Election Night 1980/Early Carter Concession: http://www
.nytimes.com/books/first/b/brinkley-unfinished.html.

4. 2008 Bush-Obama Transition: http://www.upi.com/Top
_News/2008/11/09/Obama-Bush-transition-called-smooth/
UPI-20571226242368/.

5. Hoover-FDR Transition: http://blogs.reuters.com/great-de
bate/2008/11/14/transition-lessons-from-fdr/.

6. Clinton-Bush Transition Vandalism: http://www.nytimes
.com/2002/06/12/us/white-house-vandalized-in-transition
-gao-finds.html.

7. New Congress Sworn In, Passed Legislation Before Obama
Took Office: http://articles.cnn.com/2009-01-14/politics/schip
_1_schip-bill-affordable-health-care-rep-dave-camp?
_s=PM:POLITICS.

6. INAUGURATION DAY

1. Chief Justice Roberts Flubs Obama Oath of Office: http://
www.msnbc.msn.com/id/28780417/ns/politics-white_house/.

2. JFK Inaugural: http://www.jfklibrary.org/Asset-Viewer/BqXIEM9F4024ntFl7SVAjA.aspx.

3. FDR 1945 Inaugural: http://millercenter.org/scripps/archive/speeches/detail/3337.

4. Source for Reagan 1981 Inaugural: http://www.reagan.utexas.edu/archives/speeches/1981/12081a.htm.

5. Theodore Roosevelt Inaugural: http://www.bartleby.com/124/pres42.html.

INDEX